SPARKS—TASTIC

SPARKS—TASTIC

TWENTY—ONE NIGHTS WITH SPARKS IN LONDON

TOSH BERMAN

A Barnacle Book Rare Bird Books

New York | Los Angeles

THIS IS A GENUINE BARNACLE BOOK

A Barnacle Book | Rare Bird Books
453 South Spring Street, Suite 531
Los Angeles, CA 90013
abarnaclebook.com
rarebirdbooks.com

Set in Goudy Old Style
Printed in the United States of America
Distributed in the U.S. by Publishers Group West
Photos used with permission from Ron Mael and Russell Mael

10 9 8 7 6 5 4 3 2 1

Publisher's Cataloging-in-Publication data
Berman, Tosh.
    Sparks-tastic : twenty-one nights with Sparks in London /
Tosh Berman.   p. cm.
    ISBN 9780983925583

1. Sparks (Musical group). 2. Sparks (Musical group)—Travel—England—London. 3. Sparks (Musical group)—Travel—
France—Paris. 4. Rock musicians—United States. 5. Rock
musicians—Travel—England—London. 6. Rock musicians—
Travel—France—Paris. I. Sparks-tastic : 21 nights with Sparks
in London. II. Title.

ML421.S664 B45 2013
782.42166—dc23

My wish is that you may be loved to the point of madness.
—André Breton

This book would not have happened without...

A special thanks to Amelia Cone for bringing her Sparks biography project to my attention. That book hasn't happened (yet) but it led me to writing my own book, and that wouldn't have happened without many long discussions between me and Amelia about Sparks.

Thank you Josephine Tran and Bethany Handler for reading and looking over the manuscript. Your comments were extremely helpful and kept me focused on the narrative of the book. Also, I treasure our long conversations and notes from the two of you.

Tyson Cornell, Julia Callahan, Alice Marsh-Elmer, Marina Dundjerski, and Chiwan Choi for their surgical skills in making this manuscript purr.

Thank you to Rosa and Oscar Brogden for taking care of me in Hampstead Heath and giving me the attic room to write. It was a beautiful room and your presence was a great joy and comfort. And a great thank you to Mark Webber, for allowing me to stay at his home in Kentish Town, as well as being great company. Bean...on toast? Imagine!

To my mother Shirley Berman and Uncle Donald Morand, who came with me to Paris. It truly was the saddest moment in my life when you left Paris to go back home. The hotel seemed vacant after you left.

I also want to thank two characters in the book: Paris and, especially, London. Individuals are important, but one cannot forget the weather, the architecture, and the citizens of the capital. The writings of Patrick Hamilton, Iain Sinclair, George Orwell, and André Breton's Nadja *for being very much part of my landscape while I was writing this book.*

Special love to my wife Lun*na Menoh, not only for the front cover painting, but also for encouraging me to do the impossible.

And a special thank you to the fantastic musicians Steve Nistor, Jim Wilson, Marcus Blake, Steven McDonald, and Tammy Glover.

And, of course, to Ron Mael and Russell Mael for making great art to have in my life and others...

Dear Readers and Lookie-Loos,

This is a book about Sparks, but filtered through my personal observations and obsessions. It is not a biography of a band, nor about the background of putting together a Sparks show. My main interest is my fixation with Ron Mael's and Russell Mael's music and what bounces from that medium to yours truly. Also, writing this book was a good excuse for me to spend time in London.

INTRODUCTION

A STRANGE OBSESSION

What is the meaning of this strange obsession? It's said that a man is defined by his work and friends. To me, a man is defined by his record and book collection. And, of course, the appreciation of the right type of fabric at the right time and place—Levi's button-up 501s with the cuffs up an inch (enough to see the sock)—that's pretty much all that's needed for a man in the twenty-first century, right? Well, *that*...and the twenty-one albums by Sparks.

So, when I hear that my all-time favorite group (or *obsession*)—Sparks—is doing a series of twenty-one shows in London, each night devoted to a different one of their twenty-one albums, I think there's absolutely no way I can miss this. But when I sit down to see what the trip might cost, it's obvious that there wouldn't be any possible way to make it. Then, just to be sure, I check again. Then again to be triple sure. By now, I'm quite secure with the fact that I can't possibly afford to go to London for this once-in-a-lifetime opportunity. I consider myself a responsible adult with a full-time job at a bookstore that my tax guy calls a hobby, and my publishing empire, TamTam Books. So, figuring my job and my additional career as a publisher of contemporary French literature that ninety-five percent of the population doesn't care about, I realize that I really don't make enough money to make this happen no matter how hard I try to convince myself that it *could* happen.

Have you ever *worked* at a bookstore? Not counting a time when you worked part time while you were in school or abstractly as a writer immersing yourself in the atmosphere of books—but as a *professional* bookseller working full time to support yourself because that's the career path that you've chosen? It's the kind of life that can be counted as seasons go by—literally—because that's how *professional* booksellers go through life...by the catalog seasons that books are released. Valentine's Day, Mother's Day, Father's Day, Fourth of July, Halloween, and then the ultimate season for the book buyers—Christmas. One measures the whole year and the four seasons when working full time as a professional bookseller. I really don't have the time for twenty-one days in London to hear and see twenty-one nights of Sparks.

Aside from Sparks, though, the number twenty-one keeps me attached to the idea of going. It seems to be a magic number that is calling out to me. And it dawns on me all of sudden that I live in the twenty-first century. (For whatever reason, my head is really into the twentieth century.) In the U.K., the twenty-one gun salute is especially marked for royalty; for the city of London, it is always a twenty-one gun salute. There are so many songs and book titles that have the number twenty-one (hardly any with twenty or twenty-two). And when I think of Sparks having twenty-one albums and doing twenty-one shows, man, that really stands out. It just rolls off the tongue and seems impressive. And the truth is, it really *is* impressive for a group to have twenty-one albums in their career and still carry on as if there's no end in sight.

I am also fascinated with the idea of *writing* about this experience of seeing Sparks. And it is obvious to me that I need to capture this experience on the page. A reasonable person, I guess, might fantasize about going to the shows, taking a few pictures, and jotting down a few notes. But I am an *obsessed* fan, and a book person. I need to explore all of this in words, book-length words. Sure, a picture can capture something that may take a thousand words to convey, but it can also be misinterpreted. Words expose the space between the letters and the joining of our careers as musicians (Sparks) and booksellers (Me).

There just *has* to be a way to make this happen. I need to sacrifice all, go into debt, and jeopardize the stability of my life. But it all slowly reveals itself as an inevitability. I speak to my wife, Lun*na. She says: "You *have* to go, Tosh. It's a once-in-a-lifetime experience." Those were the exact words I needed to convince me that I am not delusional (even though I am). Lun*na knows me like she knows every cinema house that's playing Yakuza flicks in Tokyo. And that phrase...*once-in-a-lifetime*. It's dangerously similar to putting a red flag in front of an angry bull.

So, do I go? Or do I falter and shake in front of mommy/daddy faith? Again, I look at the calculations on paper that scream at me: *No way you can afford to do this! You're insane to even consider it!* With that logic running through my head, I choose to do what any reasonable person should do in this situation: *Go!* To do otherwise would be non-participatory with the world of greatness.

THE NEXT MORNING, AFTER a series of severe nightmares (my subconscious is always trying to tell me what to do), I realize I've made a huge mistake. But mistakes, at least in my life, always tend to lead to greater things. This is what I want to do with my life at the tender age of fifty-three (and a half). It's now or never, and "never" has never really been a Tosh Berman modus operandi when it comes to desire. This particular desire needs to be fulfilled: the desire to follow the Mael brothers—Sparks—and see all twenty-one of their miraculous shows in London. In other words, I am either a stalker or an overaged groupie.

You may ask what kind of madness makes one actually go to all these shows? But then again—what kind of madness would lead Sparks to remember over 253 songs and put on a somewhat elaborate stage show anyway? Who's the real obsessive one, here?

The Sparks World vs. The Real World

THE SPARKS WORLD IS an obsessive group of individuals. Only a band like Sparks can conceive such a fan base that is willing to follow them to the edge of a cliff and back again onto solid ground. I don't think my obsessive friend Brian could go see his God, Morrissey, for twenty-one shows in a row. (*And he never shuts up about the wisdom of King Morrissey!*) The bitter truth is that both Brian and I are compulsive types, and I think Morrissey and Sparks simply attract such fans. Not in a dangerous or creepy sense, but more to the fact that their dedicated fans spend a great deal of their days thinking about the pop titans of their inner bedroom. With respect to Sparks, I know I do.

I have been thinking about Sparks since 1974. Which means the band has been on my mind since I was twenty years old, but with a fifteen-year-old mentality. Twenty going on fifteen, in other words. Anywhere except twenty-one (and there's that number again). I had a real fear of growing up after hearing a nasty rumor that one had to find a job—or worse, a *career*—to be an adult. I didn't want to think about any of that. But everyone around me was thinking it, and that was a hard position to be in when I wasn't sure what direction I wanted to go. In other words, I was a very spoiled teenager. I never had a teenage type of job, like babysitting or working in a supermarket. Nor did I go to college, except junior college to take a film history class, watch films, and hopefully find an obsessive art film girl. I later learned that lots of girls hang out at bookstores, which led me to an almost lifelong employment at such a place. I stayed even after I got married.

Way before that, though, I went to beauty school because my dad—in an odd but rational moment for him—thought it would be a good idea for me to learn a trade of some sort. And since my uncle was (and still is) a successful hair-dresser to the stars, it seemed obvious at the time that I would step into his shoes. Or, at the very least, be an assistant to him. *Wrong.*

One of the biggest mistakes to make when you *are* useless is attempt to prove to someone that you are *not* useless. Showing up at beauty school was no problem. My problem was washing other peoples' hair. There's a technique of lifting and holding the nape of the neck to wash underneath the hair. Every time I performed this somewhat simple act, I turned some poor

woman's back into a lukewarm bath of soapy water. Luckily the customers, mostly older women
on fixed incomes, sign an agreement stating that
they won't sue the beauty school for any reason.
The real issue I had to face was (and still is in
certain social situations) that I was clumsy, and
that I had not a clue in my head nor the hands
for dealing with someone else's hair—or even the
hair on a mannequin's head.

After being turned down by customers due to
my reputation that somehow spread to various senior women's health clinics and rest homes, the
school's administration insisted I train only on
dummy heads—and under no circumstances was I
allowed to get close to a living, paying customer. So
I spent nearly eight hours every day trying to give
dummy heads proper shampoo jobs and perms.
After two or three months of this—destroying a
good amount of mannequin heads—the instruc-
tors pulled me aside and told me it would be best
if I left the school because there was no chance in
hell they would be able to train me to be a hair-
dresser, or—even if they were able to teach me this
craft—assist in placing me with an employer that
would be willing to take a chance on me.

I was, of course, crushed, having thought
for sure I could turn my fortune around and do

something that would make me part of the employed human race, and the simple fact that I tried so hard and failed was an enormous blow to my self-confidence. It was at this time that I realized my role in life should be that of a pauper prince. I would let others take care of me while I did things of a *higher* form. I just didn't know what that *higher* form would turn out to be. Or how I would pay for it.

Never Separate The Image Of Sparks From The Music Of Sparks; Or, The Duality Of The Brother Duo

SPARKS WAS A BAND whose members somehow said to me: "Tosh, we understand what you are going through, and although your life is pure hell (and, frankly, useless), we can at least make a suitable soundtrack to your miserable situation." Although the Mael Brothers never literally said those words to me, it's what was being disseminated to me through their music—a soundtrack for me as I try to figure things out, or at the very least a chance for something else to figure things out for me. And since we're talking about pop music, we're also talking about image—how one lives out a life that is also an image, while also projecting that image to the outside world.

This is why I've always firmly believed that one should never separate the image of a band or artist from their music. The two go together like a slice of lemon in a cup of herbal tea. All music has a sort of visual image attached to it, and the visual aspect of Sparks is extremely important in supporting their musical vision.

With this, there are various dualities in the Sparks makeup. One is the brother image: the iconic cliché, the very typical relationship between biological brothers in a rock and roll band is practically made up by the fact that they are total enemies against each other. Consider Oasis, The Kinks, The Black Crowes, and The Everly Brothers. Even the great Burnette Brothers were known to knock each others' heads around with their instruments of choice. On the other side of the coin, there were brother duos like the Kray Twins, who as mobsters ruled East London in the sixties. They were never known to argue, and essentially used a secret form of communication between the two of them.

Even though Ron Mael and his younger brother Russell—the brother duo that is Sparks— have strong individual personalities, they work together in a very complementary, well-oiled machine-type of way. There are other duo art teams that, I guess, should also be addressed here in order to understand precisely how the Mael Brothers have evolved into their signature Sparks form. Two important ones are the Starn Twins and Gilbert & George. Ron and Russell Mael work very intimately with the Kray/Starn/Gilbert & George mode of brother duo maneuverings. This isn't to say that they are criminals (at least that I'm aware of)—or twins, for that matter—but it's the idea that they think of themselves, creatively, as a singular unit.

The beauty of this relationship is that the Mael Brothers understand their own unified character and how to play that role in Sparks. Ron and Russell are *both* credited with the songwriting of Sparks' later period compositions, so the responsibilities are blurred in who does what. I have never seen or read an interview where they reveal how Sparks' music is actually made. It's always been a bit of a mystery, but I guess that's what I also find intriguing. Like the Krays and Gilbert & George, they operate as one. We never hear of disagreements or arguments within the framework of their work; nor do we hear of disruptions in their private lives—which is basically off limits to the press and their fans. Ron and Russell just seem to be comfortable, not only in their own skin, but also with the fact that they share that comfort with each other. It's very much them against the world.

INTERESTING TO NOTE, TOO—NOW that I've put his fans' obsessions in with the fanaticism of Sparks' devotees—is that Morrissey is apparently a big Sparks fan, and an admirer of those other brothers-in-arms, the Krays. I think he sees them all as outsiders bound together, a force against a rather hostile world. Morrissey clearly sees the world in heroic terms; and, likewise, he's in love with the anthropology of pop and its culture. That's a big part of the Sparks' world: the mythology of their band and how they see and appreciate that world.

If one created a symbolic portrait of Sparks, they would see images of early Kinks, early Who, the great silent movie comedians, sixties French pop icons, British Music Hall artists, and the more eccentric aspects of British glam rock. It's a world that doesn't naturally fit in with whatever is happening at any particular moment. In fact, it's perpetually at odds with the current pop world.

At times I wonder if I am attracted to brothers because I don't have a brother. Or even a sister. I don't miss having a sibling. But then, I have been obsessed with images of twins and very close brothers for a long time. I've been reading and studying up on the Kray Twins and—no, I don't idolize them—I realize they're sadistic killers, but I'm fascinated with how they use their double identity in their work. Gilbert & George do the same. Both of these East London couples are stronger together than separate. And they have always realized that. Sparks, I presume, must have become conscious of this as well. I, on the other hand, only have myself. Well, me and my wife, to be specific. She's shorter than me, and Asian, while I just look like a white, middle-aged guy. It doesn't have the same visual effect as Gilbert & George, Sparks, and—without a doubt—the Kray Twins.

This image of Sparks, though, is very well worked out. There isn't a huge age difference between the brothers. Ron assumes the role of an older man by taking on the visual identity of a man from the past with a carefully trimmed mustache, slicked black hair, conservative clothing, and quiet demeanor; yet there's a certain amount of indescribable tension in his eyes. Russell, on the other hand, is a slightly eccentric version of a pop star with his hair and collection of loud jackets. He's the friendly face of the band, but he too has darkness in his eyes. What am I talking about? Both brothers have very strong eyes. And I am not referring to the theatrical way Ron moves his eyes up and down and around onstage. If you just look at the photographs, their eyes express something hidden and deep. Like their music, there's a layer of something very serious—but it's sort of back in one's brain. You want to say it, but you can't find the words to express what it is. What do I think is there? Pain.

As a listener, especially when I was nineteen, that's what I pick up on: the pain of being the fool in the crowd, a loser in romance, not in the swing of things, and basically stuck in a very gray world. Sparks' inner world is like a world of Technicolor, widescreen, and on 70mm film. Yet one gets the feeling that it, too, probably came from a gray area of the world, and therefore had to remake it into something else. A better world of sorts. But there are still these nagging doubts about life and these people imposing their mediocre thoughts, their petty and boring way of dress, and just the nature of living in a world that is too, too real.

Glam rock made perfect sense to me at the time because it was a world made up. Just add makeup and you're on your way. But for me, personally, makeup was a tad too exotic. There were aspects of it I liked a lot, but there was also something inelegant about glam. It was too drag artistry for my taste. I love and admire that world but it's never been a style that I naturally aligned myself to rock on a day-to-day basis. Ron and Russell, though, had a style that appealed to me the first moment that I saw *Kimono My House*.

The image they took had wider implications. I was mostly intrigued by Ron's style. His songs dealt with youthful angst, but his appearance was somewhat older—a perverted older man, one could say. He also didn't look American, more European—even a cross between a British Music Hall performer and a Munich citizen from the thirties. The juxtaposition of music and image was really shocking to me at the time. And having Russell being *sort of* the standard pop image of a lead singer made the mix even stranger. The very visual image of Sparks makes them quite different from all other bands. Even John Lennon, the wit he was, while watching them on *Top of the Pops*, had to announce: "Hey, look, Hitler's in a band." Ron's mustache often gave people that reaction.

To this day, most people think Sparks hails from Europe. One guy even tried to convince me they came from New York City. True fans know Sparks is from Southern California, though.

Was there something in the water? Their genes? What we know of their family is nothing, maybe a few rumors. One big rumor is that they were child models for Sears, but this hasn't been officially confirmed or denied. Also, the "Mary Martin" listed as the president of the Sparks Fan Club is actually reported to be their mother. Again, this hasn't been confirmed or denied. But one has to love the idea that the President of the Sparks Fan Club for the past thirty years is the one who literally gave birth to them. And isn't that also the name of the great stage actress who haunted me as a kid by playing Peter Pan?

The beauty of Sparks—or *a* beautiful aspect of Sparks—is that one never truly is sure of Sparks' backstory. And, as a fan, I don't want to know. I enjoy all the legends. Like, was Russell on his high school football team? Were the Mael brothers in the audience at the filmed *T.A.M.I./T.N.T. Show* in 1964? Were they actually models in their youth? The stories change on a consistent basis. What may seem true seemingly becomes an urban myth...but then you find out something else that makes you think it's really truth again. Then again, is truth really applicable to the world of Sparks? I think not. It's what is conveyed through the music and image that is more important than a life history that seems truthful. Do we need to know if the brothers are married? Gay or straight? Or if they are even real brothers?

No, all of that truth-seeking doesn't matter. It's the narration that is laid out in front of us, and how we take it as a form of truth. But we also realize that there are many levels of truth. This is not only an observation of Sparks, but also an observation of everything that is in front of us on this planet. We, as consumers, simply digest this information that is delivered to us. Sparks curates a world of its own making. Ron and Russell are, fundamentally, an entrance to a world that is somehow or somewhat better than the actual world we live in. The Sparks landscape is a world full of doubt, pain, and Peter Pan. We're all in love with Wendy—but we'll never connect with her. And that, simply put, is the tension and humor taking place in every Sparks song ever created.

This is the ideal love that I have for Sparks that's so appealing to me. You can almost touch it, but you can't actually hold it. The essence of the band's genius is on the tip of your fingertips, but you can't feel it. Sparks songs are a world within themselves, but a fragile world with intensity as a form of purity—where Kafka meets James Thurber, perhaps.

Love Them Or...Don't Get Them At All

I HAVE TWO SETS of friends: one set who is totally into Sparks, and another set who doesn't get them at all. One of the criticisms of those who don't get them is the supposed *artificiality* of their music. The pop world naturally conveys a sort of unreality to their stars, though. On one hand, you have bands that can be read intention-wise a mile away. This is probably true for almost every indie rock artist. Yet, for most music fans, that's exactly what's appealing and what makes them *comfortable* with the act. Sparks has a lot going on, and to really appreciate the music you have to be in tune with the band's aesthetics and humor. That's generally a lot to ask of an audience, though. It means the audience has to actually think to appreciate. Or at least put two and two together in their head. It might not quite add up to four. Maybe three. But it's in those miscalculations where unique and uncompromising bands like Sparks live out the essence of their work.

However, the irony of this "difficult" group is that Sparks writes the strongest melodies possible in a pop musics format. Usually two or three melodic lines in one song, which can often be too much for a listener who wants their entertainment spoon-fed and in easy, palatable bites. Sparks doesn't cut up its food, musically speaking, for easy digestion. The Mael Brothers are in the driver's seat, they're going to take you for a wild ride—and how that ride is going to end up is a complete and total mystery. You just have to trust that they know what they're doing, and they don't make any wrong turns along the way.

Before this retrospective of twenty-one shows, I had been under the assumption that Sparks *had* made a series of wrong turns. For instance, the albums *Introducing Sparks, Music That You Can Dance To,* and *Pulling Rabbits Out Of The Hat.* Fatal car accidents were more like what I would use to describe my feeling about these albums, but after experiencing these twenty-one shows, I've been enlightened. The recordings are still weak to my ears, but the songs done live (with no arrangement changes) swing and sing out to me in glorious visions of pure bliss. And on top of that, I have no way of guessing what the sound will be like for the *next* album. I know the voice, the lyrical bent of the subject matter, but the sound varies wildly from album to album. Always quirky is a reasonable expectation, but where Sparks takes you is often not on any map.

And now, ladies and gentleman, we are about to go into the belly of the beast that is Sparks—but also into my rather fragile mental state. I am far away from TamTam Books—and my wife; I miss her dearly. I realize that I have trouble sleeping when she's not around. She has bleach-blonde hair, and I miss the smell of her hair while sleeping. Usually, my head is in her piled hair to lure sweet dreams, but without her and the hair, it can be a troublesome period of time in bed. One wonders if I can find a pillow that smells like hair bleach, because that may solve my sleeping problem.

To make sure, though, that I will not chicken out, I write to Ron and Russell Mael to let them know I am flying to London to see all of their shows—and, even more importantly, to write a book about the experience. Then I brag to all my fellow coworkers that I am going to London to write a book. Even my local postman knows that I am going to London. So, now making a stand of sorts, I have to go. Thinking about something like this is one thing, but once you tell someone you are going to do something—that's when it becomes real.

Swinging London

EVERYONE IN MY GENERATION, I think, discovered the U.K. via the Beatles. They were walking pictures of what English life was like, or imagined to be like, by us Americans. It was exotic, but felt like home because they spoke something similar to our language. Beyond that, they even looked better than us Americans. I don't know what it was, I guess, a certain flair of sorts. I do know that if a young girl thought you were British in the early sixties it meant you were either super smart or great looking. And that was something I often desired.

As I got older, the city of London grew only more compelling to me, due mostly to a culture and aesthetic value I thought *was* London. Basically, London to *me* is a place that may not exist. And though I have been there numerous times, to this day it's still sort of like a fantasyland where I read only what I choose to read in its buildings, people, and maps. Like Raymond Roussel, I could have stayed in my room on a luxury liner and just imagined what London was like.

I got *my* London via the movies of Joseph Losey and Donald Cammell, as well as literature by Patrick Hamilton and Colin Macinnes' very realistic and gritty novel, *Absolute Beginners*. This fantastic book exposed an aspect of London culture not known to me at the time. It takes place in the fifties, and was probably one of the first novels to deal with the multicultural side of life in the capital during that era—as well as being the first novel to deal with the concept of the teenager. A mod landmark in literature, it has always stayed in my mind whenever I visited London.

My wife Lun*na, as I mentioned before, encouraged me to go on this trip. (I'm not sure if it's because she needs the extra space in our house.) Lun*na also has no fear of financial ruin or insecurities regarding being homeless and totally broke. Her spirit is one that says: *You can do it!* To have total success with her is great, but failure is not so bad with her around as well. She seems to be excited that I am going, but the truth is that the thought of her not going with me gives my heart a terrible ache. So I try not to think about it. It's sort of like when one leaves the household for the first time to go camping with other kids. (Which, by the way, I have never done.)

As an only child, I was pretty much left alone to amuse myself. Records were (and still are) very much my true friends. I bought a lot of teen magazines when I was around ten, and my bedroom walls were covered from top to bottom with photos from them of various individuals. I had one huge Beatles poster with their autographs (printed on the poster) posing in front of a British doorway. Beyond that there were photos of almost every British Invasion band in existence. From the Dave Clark Five to Dave Berry. The only girl I had on my wall was a series of images of Haley Mills, a British teen actress, my first serious love and the only love of my preteen years. She expressed a world that I didn't know about but wanted desperately to go into, cosmically. And I guess Sparks took me to a world that I now think we shared. Somewhere between Neverland and Central London.

It was two or three years before my father's death when I first got into Sparks. The album that turned my head into mush, as I alluded to before, was *Kimono My House*. I must have seen Sparks photos in British publications like *New*

Music Express or *Melody Maker*. At the time, I refused to even look at American rock and roll magazines. Their aesthetic didn't do it for me—and, basically, I was a hardcore glam fan. As I mentioned, I didn't wear makeup (except for face powder—Johnson & Johnson, if memory serves me correctly). But it was done very subtly. I didn't do it to look more feminine. Just to add to my already pretty white skin, making it even whiter. I was struck by looking at myself in the mirror and having my face caked in white powder, which made my lips look really red in comparison with the rest of the face. Without a doubt I was the only teenager that had this look in Topanga Canyon, where I grew up. In the valley, maybe there were two or three guys with that kind of look, but for sure in Topanga I held the only patent. My role models at the time were probably Kraftwerk during their incredible *Trans-Europe Express* period. They adopted their look as Berlin in the thirties. Totally retro, but with electronic instruments. The juxtaposition was similar to Ron Mael—where he represented the past but his actions were totally into the now, or even in the future. The German fab four introduced me to the pleasures of cultural history, but Sparks pushed me to actually get my Jimmy

Page-length hair cut off. I wanted to visually belong to another era, yet even be more modern than possible. That's really the definition and philosophy of mod, right?

Like I said, though, the first picture I saw of Ron and Russell was the back cover of *Kimono My House*. I was struck by the duality of Ron Mael's Hitler-or-is-it-Chaplin mustache and Russell's classic good looks with sharp cheeks and intense eyes. They played their identities off each other well. I sensed new adventure just looking at that one photo. It was then that I felt I had found an entrance to a world I needed to go to. The image was just a spotlight on the brothers, and I thought that was so dramatic at the time. An article I read mentioned that when Sparks played live the only lighting required was a single spotlight on Ron and Russell, the rest of the band in blackness. I wanted to enter the image.

The thing is, I can never match the vision and scope of this special world that is Sparks. I can sit in the audience, I can buy the records, and purchase magazines with articles on them— but never could I match the brilliance of their look or visuals with the music. In many ways it confuses me more when I consider Sparks and what I should do with my life. They're so special, and I'm just *kind* of special, but I'm nowhere near the genius level that makes Sparks work. What I get out of it is that I need to change the world that I live in. For better or worse, Sparks is throwing bread crumbs on the road and I am following those crumbs as closely as possible.

I bought *Kimono My House* at the Warehouse, a horrible record store in Woodland Hills, and it may have been an import from England—so the price was like $3.99, instead of the regular $2.49 LP price. So it was an investment made only going by the image of these two brothers. I couldn't imagine the sounds of the music on the album being terrible. That never even entered my mind. The image was too good.

So I got home and put on side one with "This Town Ain't Big Enough For The Both Of Us," the first song, and was...totally...and...completely...destroyed. To this day, I've yet to hear a recording so strange and powerful. It was chaos made by a strong melody and an insane beat. A gallop of sorts. I wondered how many galloping horses could possibly be put in a recording studio. It was that visual image, yet given aurally. I didn't even know what the song was about. Hell, I couldn't even grasp at what Russell was singing about because he was singing the lyrics at 200-plus miles per hour. He was cramming so many words into a three-minute-and-something-second song.

But it wasn't only that one song. The next one devastated me as well. And then the next. By the end of side two I felt as if I had heard and seen something truly remarkable. With Kraftwerk in the rear view mirror, and Ron ignoring the seventies, it was the time of *Propaganda*, their fourth album, that made me change my Jimmy Page style into what I thought was the modern man. It was at this point that I started to slick my thick black hair in the style of Ron Mael. I didn't grow the mustache because I didn't have the courage to do so. Still, the music of Sparks encouraged me to go after my own identity. I just used Ron as the prototype to a new look. So basically for the next five or six years I would wear only suits with slicked back hair. To me, it wasn't just a look. It was an identity change to say that I was not the same person I was during the first half of my life. Because that side of the world had failed me completely. Eventually my dad's death in 1976 made a very strong line in the sand for me, and to live as an identity that I made had to be emphasized in drastic changes.

But then I realized that there had to be a change or I would just, in a way, live life in a world without *my* own making.

Discovering Sparks' *Kimono My House* was sort of a coin that was thrown in the air and one that landed right in front of me. Heads was the image of the front cover with the two Japanese girls, and tails was the portrait of Ron and Russell (with the rest of the band). I chose tails. That image of them liberated me from a particular mindset I was in at the time. I needed the duality that was expressed in this clothing of Sparks. If I had chosen heads, I guess I might be dressing like a Japanese girl in a kimono.

Topanga Canyon and The Sparks Aesthetic

TO FULLY UNDERSTAND NOW, you have to imagine what life was like in the early seventies. There were essentially two sides of rock and roll being made in Los Angeles, and I was surrounded by a canyon area politely called Topanga Canyon. (My Topanga Canyon moniker-of-choice was "Top-of-the-Pain-GA Canyon.") On one side was the very talented Neil Young. On the other side, there was Charles Manson, the street sadistic thug turned idol of scary. Then, there was Sunset Boulevard and a club called Rodney Bingenheimer's English Disco. One didn't see Neil Young or Charles Manson at this teeny-bop heaven. They saw glam rock in all its glitter and glory, with miles of cute girls to match the guys in platform shoes and patent leather pants.

The tragedy was that the cute girls were there for the older, flashier guys, like members of Led Zeppelin, Spiders from Mars, The Stooges, and other great icons of the time who put a touch of makeup around the eyes and had a common penchant for the young and teenage. It was an interesting scene on a lot of levels, especially with the English Disco's very own overage teenager, Rodney Bingenheimer, flocking with his usual and endless supply of young girls deeply interested in this culture of music, musicians, and the experiential aspects of that combination. It was both great and awful to witness the spectacle that was Rodney and his English Disco.

The problem was that I didn't seem to be attractive enough or cute enough to reel these girls in. Whatever it was about the San Fernando Valley's water supply or the handsome men and women who breed and move to the area, there was no doubt an extremely large population of beautiful girls in my high school. And the ones I was interested in were all into the glam aesthetic. They liked the men under the makeup, but it was an aesthetic that wasn't really taking place in Topanga.

The Sparks aesthetic had nothing in common with Topanga Canyon. I found the world away from my home way more interesting due that it was a fresh approach to a life that can be different and as artificial as factory-made candy. Canyon life was a reality that was pretty much set by a Neil Young stoner attitude mixed in with Charles Manson's view of a better world that would be a disaster. Sparks, in this same way, was a sense of lightness mixed with a very twisted dark edge.

SPARKS' NEXT ALBUM, PROPAGANDA, this time purchased by my parents, sold me a new lifestyle. It was, in a spiritual sense, a goodbye to the post-hippie world of Topanga. Which, after a while, became conservative and not so forward-thinking. Sparks represented a world that never really became tiring. It was French new wave films, Jacques Tati, endless amounts of ice cream, and beautiful girls that one could see at a distance but could never touch.

At this point in my life, I needed to be in *that* world. Not away from my parents, who were always supportive of me, but from the old rules of a social environment which was clearly not working for me. I wasn't rebelling against the world because I felt the world was rebelling against me.

The main tragedy, however, was my father's death in 1976. His passing didn't necessary stop time, but it made me feel that there was no time left. I became obsessive about the pacing of the day. Did I write enough poems for the day? Or see enough films during the week? Always a bookworm, I then refused to leave the house without a book in my hand. In one way, it was a fashion accessory. But on a deeper level, it was an object that made me feel connected to a world that didn't belong to anyone else except me. My books, to this very day, represent who I truly am. When I'm speaking to you, it's a front to simply make it through the day. When I carry a book, that book is who I really am.

One of the reasons why I love working in the bookstore is that it's a daily performance in front of customers and fellow coworkers. This is true for most or all retail, I guess. I wouldn't know the real me if it bit me in the ass—and I don't necessarily care to—it's the unreal that's so much more interesting. The façade is more beautiful than the foundation. Sparks is embracing of the façade, and it's how the brothers use their canvas that makes their art so fascinating. They aren't from Europe, but they sound European. Perhaps even Viennese. How the hell is Sparks from Southern California? Who gives a fuck? The reality is that they made up a world that suits them and their aesthetic. And to appreciate them, we all have to realize that the façade is the medium where they choose to live out their art.

RUSSELL MAEL CAME IN to the bookstore where I worked to get a book gift-wrapped. It was sort of a horrible moment for me, because I wanted to acknowledge him as one of my all-time favorite singers in one of the greatest bands of all time. But I also wanted him to write the introduction for my then upcoming Gainsbourg publication. In my heart, I just felt that there was a need for him to get involved in my project. Re-reading this last sentence, it does sound kind of creepy, but I knew I only had thirty seconds to confront him with my various passions. I thought hard for ten seconds and then said, "I am a huge fan of your work, and by the way...do you like Serge Gainsbourg?"

He said "Yes" and "Thank you" at the same time. He then mentioned having met Gains-bourg. I asked him right there if he would write an introduction to *Evguenie Sokolov*. When you only have seconds, one has to move fast, even with the possibility of total embarrassing fail-ure.

Russell gave me his mailing address and I sent him the manuscript. Within a month he came back with his great introduction. A friend-ship started with a close friend of his, Amelia Cone (I love her name), and we worked togeth-er on a Sparks' book project that didn't happen due to finances. But it started the ball rolling in my court to actually do a book on Sparks. This is that book.

The first thing I did when I realized I was going to write this book was buy a laptop com-puter; on the same day, I downloaded my entire Sparks collection on iTunes. The only album I didn't have was *Interior Design* (now released). I decided to worry about that later, right then I had to focus on the psychological root of my problems and why they were leading me toward this particular adventure. The only answer I could think of was that I was crazy.

I EVEN RAN INTO Morrissey at my work and although I didn't know him, I told him that I
would be going to London to see all twenty-one
concerts of Sparks. His first comment was, "I
don't believe you." Then his second comment
was, "You're crazy."

THE THING IS I have no money and right now the
dollar is so low it barely even registers on the eco-
nomic front. Also I can't afford to leave my job,
nor my work with TamTam Books. And I will
miss my wife. Will she change my home office
into her office? Lots of insecure feelings about
insecure things. There are only three things in
life that are true: death, taxes, and regret.

PARIS

JARDIN DES PLANTES

went to London following a wonderful yet stressful stay in Paris. As things happen, I was invited to the opening of a huge exhibition at the Centre Pompidou called *Traces du Sacré*. My mom and uncle were also invited to this show because my dad, the artist Wallace Berman, had a few art pieces in it. Uncle Donald invited his friend Yuki to come along on the trip as well. I was nervous regarding my mother's and uncle's comfort in a foreign country. I was also nervous about Yuki because he is a high class guy with high class taste—and with respect to travel, I am about two levels below Jack Kerouac. Yuki was more of the Paul Bowles traveler with sixteen suitcases and a small carpet to make himself feel at home. My packing for both Paris and London was a small suitcase full of black t-shirts (seven days worth) and my computer case carrying the brand new MacBook.

The honor of going to this exhibit meant I had to change my travel plans, which means instead of going to London directly I flew to Paris with my family (and Donald's best friend) and stayed there for a week or so before heading to London on the Eurostar. All manageable. At least at the time I thought so.

I was never made out to be a travel agent, yet with help from a travel agency I did my best for a senior citizen brother and sister who like to smoke in a world that doesn't smoke anymore, including finding a hotel where they could smoke without getting in trouble. Like the rest of the world, Paris is slowly eliminating *le smoke* from its restaurants and hotels. Which left my mother shaking her head at various windowsills to sneak a smoke here and there.

TRACES DU SACRÉ WAS a big deal because, along with my father, the exhibition also had artists like Picasso, Mondrian, Kandinsky, Man Ray,

Marcel Duchamp, and the king of kink and darkness, Aleister Crowley. The focus of the show was the element of spirituality in these artists' works. Some were explicit (Crowley and Kenneth Anger), and others were traces of an interest in either the spiritual world or mysticism. Even being in a first class show we still had to pay for the trip there, as well as for the nice little hotel we stayed at directly across from the dinosaur room at the Jardin des Plantes. At nighttime, the oversized and dramatically lit dinosaur skeletons would look through our window, which hopefully didn't mean bad luck for the trip.

THE ONLY PLACE WE could afford was this hotel near the Jardin des Plantes, which was not that close to the action, but close to the train and taxi station. The hotel/apartment, which in reality was a hotel without the regular service of a hotel, and perhaps a couple of Euros cheaper, had a small kitchen, two beds, two forks, two knives, one sharp kitchen knife, two coffee cups, two drinking glasses, two wine glasses, two burners on the stove, one bottle opener, and—for some strange reason—one tea spoon. Also a television set, writing desk, and a nice bathroom. But no regular service in the lobby except from

8:00 A.M. to 12:00 P.M. and 4:00 P.M. to 7:00 P.M. Which is perfectly fine, except when your flight comes in at 8:00 P.M. and you aren't sure if you have the code to get into the building; that can cause a touch of anxiety.

Nevertheless, my mom and uncle never knew my anxieties about getting inside our rooms as I just bit my lip for twelve hours on the plane. But, of course, the Tosh luck kicked in and we got into our rooms without any problems whatsoever, and to this day (until they read this book, I guess) they never did know that we may have almost had to sleep in front of the hotel door and wait for someone to let us in the next morning. My worst fear was to make my mother sleep on the nineteenth century pavement of Rue Buffon without a blanket or bed.

It was my duty to get this pair of hotel/apartments for my family, and I felt it would be a great dishonor if I didn't succeed in what many think would be a simple act. Flying over, all I could think about was the door code and what I would do if it didn't work. And I looked at my mom's face, sitting beside me in coach, and her eyes said: *Please make this plane go faster so I can get to the hotel.* Failure was not an option, but I felt there was a good chance of a total disaster.

Our stay in Paris was very moving to me on many fronts. This trip struck me as kind of sad because I felt like this could be the last time I would go on a trip like this with my family (of three).

THE HOTEL WAS WITHIN walking distance of my beloved—and now mystical—Saint-Germain-des-Prés. I could walk to all of the Boris Vian locations in the neighborhood. One of the main problems with my mom being on this trip with me is that she doesn't drink, and I need at the very least a bottle of wine every night. I have never brought this up with my doctor but I am sure he would agree that I do need the bottle every night. There is a great pleasure when one can wander off by himself slightly intoxicated and just dwell on the Parisian neighborhoods. During the night, street lighting reflects off the Seine and gives off dramatic shadows on the buildings, I can imagine the famous illustration of Fantômas taking a giant step over a building with a knife in his hand. My hands are stretched out: *Liberate me, liberate me.*

Wine, bread, and Boris Vian locations are the real reasons for going to Paris and for me the very definition of desire. All of the other stuff, like visiting the Centre Pompidou is, well, basically work. Pleasurable work yes, but nevertheless work. But to get wasted on the streets of Paris is a force that is so powerful and beautiful at the same time. Though, sadly, I didn't get wasted on this particular trip to Paris. I got buzzed, but not anywhere near wasted. I was a sober and very respectful host to my family of three, and that was my proper role here at this time and place.

IN THE HOTEL/APARTMENT ON Rue Buffon I could look directly across the street to Jardin des Plantes, a natural history museum dating back to the French Revolution. Georges-Louis Leclerc, Comte de Buffon, who was probably one of the first individuals interested in collecting both plant and animal life, built the palace and stately park. The basic premise was to have one of everything in his Jardin des Plantes, but eventually, sadly, he was executed during the French Revolution. I sat in our hotel room on the Rue Buffon and thought that Sparks, in a way, are a perverted version of Jardin des Plantes, and the Comte de Buffon.

Ron and Russell collect various emotional responses from people who are outside of the system and not part of the general world. In doing so, Sparks has become sort of a spokesperson for those who just can't. Buffon, as a scientist, just wanted to document the physical existence of animals and plants, while Sparks wants to document emotional existence.

Buffon saw a mysterious world open up to him that needed to be named and documented. Sparks is conducting a kind of science experiment by doing every album live onstage, preserving their work in a way that is archival in concept and fleeting in execution.

RECORDINGS AND LIVE MATERIAL are two different media at work. I think artists like Bob Dylan have a hard time dealing with the concept of recordings because it is a dead medium that just lies there on the ground for them. Dylan tours consistently for the sole purpose of feeling alive and making his songs breathe on a nightly basis.

With respect to Sparks, one medium serves the other. Ron and Russell, with their magnificent band—Steven Nistor on drums, Jim Wilson and Marcus Blake on guitars, and the eye-magnet, Steven McDonald on bass—reproduce the sound and arrangements of the original recordings onstage. Dylan has a need to change the songs to keep them alive and at the present, but Ron and Russell are more like Buffon in that they are documenting their work and not interested in reinterpreting the songs. It's not a question of giving the audiences what they want such as just the familiar hits, but a need for them to document their work as accurately as possible.

ON THE DAY MY mom, my uncle, and Yuki flew back to Los Angeles and left me here alone at their hotel, I decided to spend the week before the Sparks shows in Paris, to be in this city alone. I was moved to tears when my mom and the others got in the taxi and left the hotel. I went downstairs with them to say goodbye, and it felt weird that I wasn't in the car with them. Some years ago in Tokyo I went to see a Noh play about a prisoner who is taken to an island to serve his life sentence alone on this island. The whole play was the guards taking a prisoner to the island and then leaving him there. The guards (very) slowly drift away from the island. And the intensity of abandonment and loneliness palpitates through the crowd. That is how I felt when my mom left for the airport.

On our last night together, we went to a friend's penthouse apartment near the Cimetière du Père-Lachaise (Oscar Wilde's permanent home) and the view from their terrace was simply awesome. This was the second home I visited in Paris and both places have images of my father's work. One had *Semina Culture* on the living room table and this one had an image of my dad from a poster announcing an exhibition that took place in Los Angeles some years ago.

At my friend's apartment, the dinner was an elegant but simple meal. Our hostess was a vegetarian, and I suspect the only vegetarian in Paris. We had our cocktails and wine on the balcony and I was reminded again of Fantômas in his ability to walk among the slanted roofs of Paris.

Since I have been in Paris, I have not seen one door key. It seems that all the doors here in Paris have a code you must know. My notebook is full of these codes and it's difficult to place the right code with the right door, due to my disorganization.

WHEN I GOT BACK to our hotel room that night, I had the strangest dream. I was on a train with some of the girls that I work with at Book Soup and I saw Ron Mael of Sparks sitting not far from us. It seemed like he was conducting an interview with a journalist. When I approached him I said "Hi" and he said "Hi" back to me. Ron asked how I was and how the trip was going so far. I told him everything was fine. It was at this moment that I realized that it wasn't Ron Mael but someone pretending to be Ron Mael. Yet whoever he was, he was an excellent Ron Mael. This in my dream didn't disturb me in the very least. I kept up my part of the conversation as if he was Ron.

AFTER MY FAMILY LEFT I went to the Jardin du Luxembourg to sit by the *Fontaine de Médicis*. I am a huge fan of man-made parks. I don't like wilderness being wild. I like it when an architect controls the landscape. Japanese and French gardens are in that nature so I really love Jardin du Luxembourg. It looks very much like the park in the film *Last Year at Marienbad* by Alain Resnais. All the trees are perfectly cut and taken care of. There is nothing natural about this, and that gives me great comfort at looking at them. The green leaves look like they could have been hand dyed. *Fontaine de Médicis* was moved to this park sometime in the early 1800s and it is here I sit under this particular theme of voyeurism.

It fronts a wading or meditation pool where one can sit by the water way to read, to eat, or just to reflect on the statue and the park. This beautiful statue/fountain consists of a large figure looking over a pair of lovers. I think what throws me is that I always suspect a work of art from the eighteenth or nineteenth century, especially a sculpture surely has something to do with religion or a spiritual manner. But this statue seems to be fully focused on voyeurism. And I wonder why that subject matter was chosen as a work of public art in a very popular park on the Left Bank.

By coincidence, there was a pair of beauties sitting directly across from me studying the same statue. One was noir and the other was blanc—and that's all the French I know. The black girl had the beautiful skin color of gray chocolate and the white girl looked like she'd never been exposed to the sun. Both beauties were commenting on *Fontaine de Médicis* as well as pointing to a pile of paper on their laps that looks like a manuscript of some sort. I'm in awe of the beauty of watching all of this while being alone in Paris and just admiring these gorgeous young women admiring and discussing the statue. Maybe that is what the statue is about.

THIS WAS MY FIRST night as a Parisian in the sense that I was going to cook my dinner in the small kitchen in the hotel room. Before dinner I needed to go shopping for food. First, I had to find out what a market looked like in Paris. After walking for hours around Paris trying to find a Safeway, Gelson's, or even a Ralphs, I settled for a quaint food market by the train station. I found a bottle of red wine for fewer than two euros! Yes, I found the Charles Shaw of France. Two Buck Chuck is a little more expensive as Two Euro Chuck.

I VISITED THE CIMETIÈRE du Montparnasse to give my respects to Serge Gainsbourg, who I have always been obsessed with, as well as Charles Baudelaire and Tristan Tzara—two major poets who consistently have an influence in the way I think about writing and aesthetics. But first I had lunch on Boulevard du Montparnasse, and walked out an hour and a half later wonderfully drunk.

I zigzagged toward the Cimetière du Montparnasse. Compared to the other two major cemeteries, the Montparnasse graveyard is very straightforward. The roads in the cemetery go from north to south, west to east. I walked up to the tomb of Serge Gainsbourg and studied the photographs and cigarette butts that were left on the grave. There is something not too serious about the gravesite. It's not funny, but it feels almost as though his death was not taken seriously. I think that was a part of his appeal. He talked and sang about serious things in sort of an off handed way. And even in death there seems to be this showbiz aspect that separates the man from his actions.

Down a ways from the Gainsbourg site I saw a statue on a tomb that made me cry. It was a classically nude man covering his face in grief and below him is a woman blowing him a kiss as she is dragged by a ghostly figure into the underworld. But the man's grief and the deceased blowing a kiss as a last gesture as if to say: *Don't worry everything will be okay.* I stood by this statue and cried. It is one of those things that just struck a cord in me and I can't even now forget how it affected me.

I found the Baudelaire tomb, which is his family tomb. There is a famous picture of him as well as handwritten poems to him or perhaps his work hand written by fans. When I was at the gravesite, there was a man writing a poem.

Paris has two separate identities. One is in the daylight and the other late at night. When no one is around, at say 3:00 p.m. or 4:00 p.m. in the morning it has a chilling beauty to it. Especially if you are near an old Gothic church. But things are lively at nighttime, as well. The road along the Seine is a location for impromptu parties of all sorts. Lots of young people bring their instruments and PA systems and have parties. Paris is very human in the sense that people are allowed to have a good time.

I took a cab to Gare du Nord for the Eurostar to London. I found myself almost coming to tears due to leaving Paris. This trip has been very emotional already, weird since I'm not an emotional person for the most part. Something about the city of Paris brings out the emotion in me. I always had a deep feeling for Paris. I don't know why.

Perhaps it was because my father always had an image of Brigitte Bardot in his studio as well as Artaud and Cocteau. I was raised in a household that was decorated by French pop culture in the mid-twentieth century. Apparently it stuck. It is something that I breathed in through my dad's environment. The beauty of Paris will always be somehow tied in with the memory of my father.

My dad's memory is something I have to deal with on a regular basis, since I am the head of the estate. I have to think how his work should be placed in the world, which often brings up the personal memories that sometimes over-whelm me. Particularly in Paris, a city that my father never visited. I know the realities of Paris, as I have been here a handful of times, but my father had the better deal because he had Paris the way he imagined it to be. In certain ways, that's what this whole adventure is all about.

TWENTY-ONE NIGHTS

HALFNELSON/SPARKS (1972)
MAY 16, 2008
ENCORE: "ENGLAND"

B ack home, I have a collection of Sparks press
releases and photos from the early seventies. A friend of mine got them from Greg
Shaw's estate sale. They span from Sparks' first
album when they were known as Halfnelson to
the seven-inch for "Number One Song In Heav-
en." Besides the Beatles in the sixties, and Bowie
in the seventies, no other artist has moved from
one style of music to another within such a short
period of time. The only thing that Sparks has
consistently done is be quirky.

When I lay out the press releases on a table
and look at the images that go with each release,

it's quite remarkable: they haven't lost the nerve to go full-throttle for their artistic ambition. The more lost I feel in my life, the more comfortable I am in Sparks' world. The band is self-contained here, and exceedingly chaotic. With these twenty-one nights, Sparks is finally bringing order to the world.

FROM 1964 TO THE mid-seventies I would purchase a copy of *Melody Maker* at my local food market in Topanga Canyon every Thursday. Why a grocery store in Topanga would carry such a publication? I have no clue. Maybe they wanted to serve musicians living in Topanga at that time. But they only carried three copies per week, and I always bought one.

TOPANGA WAS ALIENATING FOR a teenager like me, but *Melody Maker* gave me insight into a different world, reminded me that there was a wide world outside of the small one I was currently living in. A few record stores in L.A. carried British imports, so it was occasionally possible to get some of the music that was reviewed in English papers. As little as Sparks was written about in the American music magazines, the band was constantly being written about in *Melody Maker*.

Ron and Russell are both from Los Angeles, and Sparks is an American band, but it was alienated from the American scene in many ways. Because of *Melody Maker* I got to know the music that influenced Sparks, music that wasn't being played so much in America at the time, music that I had to dig around for in funky record stores that have long since shut down.

I SPEND THE DAY of the first Sparks show checking out the Angel tube station area of Islington where Sparks is going to do its series of twenty-one shows in twenty-one nights. I used to hang out in this neighborhood some years ago. I liked it here because there were two cool record stores, which are now gone, and various restaurants. The location has since been built up and now there is a strip mall named N1, that consists of a Borders, HMV, Starbucks, and the Carling Academy, where Sparks is playing.

Walking across the street to Chapel Market from the shopping center gives a taste of the color of Islington. Chapel Market hosts a daily outside market that sells ethnic foods, bargain-priced toothpaste, soaps, used books (excellent selection by the way), luggage, and cheap toys. It is one of the few locations where I can buy a big brand name tube of toothpaste for only one pound. Surrounding this market are cafés, pubs, electronic stores, and various interior food markets.

Islington is also where the sixties record producer Joe Meek once had his studio. It's where he killed his landlady, then himself. Within walking distance of Meek's studio is the location where the Playwright Joe Orton was killed in his flat by his longtime lover, Kenneth Halliwell, with a hammer to the head.

HALFNELSON, THE ALBUM, IS the sound of a beginning, but a beginning much more advanced than anything else released in 1972. The lights go down at Carling Academy, Islington, and this first show seems to give me the distinct feeling of time passing. The band starts off shaky with "Wonder Girl," mostly due to the mix. But by the third song, "Roger," the sound system is roaring and the band is completely focused.

Tonight, we'll see if this concept has the potential to work. It'll be an awkward twenty-one nights if the first show doesn't. The crowd is full and anticipating. They know *Halfnelson*, and although every night must be its own show, this first one serves as a litmus test. How is this grand experiment going to work?

Sparks gives the audience what it wants. For some, it is just an evening's entertainment. For others, twenty-one nights of work. Of coming to every show. Standing in the audience. Going through the gamut of emotions, old and new. Every song on the stage with no surprises, no disco arrangements, no rethought versions. The original album done in the classic style. The series of shows in Islington, London are not a journey to the past, but reclamation of their work as a contemporary art making.

WHEN I ENTER THE venue I see Emmi, Russell's girlfriend, by the band's merchant table, which is sort of a Sparks supermarket of goodies. Various t-shirts, sweaters, some of their CDs (the titles that they own and put out on their own label, Lil' Beethoven), and their souvenir book, which represents their entire career. It strikes me how eccentric, obsessive, and perhaps bordering on madness it is to redo the entire Sparks catalogue onstage.

THE FIRST ALBUM I heard by Sparks was *Kimono My House*, which overwhelmed me with its mixture of sound and visual attack. Three months later I obsessively tracked down the first two albums.

Since *Kimono My House* is one of the most radical works from the seventies it is interesting to go back in chronological order to Sparks' first album. Here one hears the roots of what the band is going to do, and you know by the strong quality of the songwriting that it will never falter from this point forward.

THE SONGS ON *HALFNELSON* change in a second's notice. The opening track, "Wonder Girl," is a perfect and simple pop song. But Sparks being Sparks, when everyone is turning left, it's going right. There is an uncompromising quality in the work (even in the lesser albums). The aesthetic style is never for sale. "Wonder Girl" is a song about a special girl, but she's more of an imaginary girl than a real one. Unlike the imaginary perfect girls of other pop songs, a farting sound toward the end of the song somehow conveys that maybe the girl is not as wonderful as originally expressed. As usual there is a duality in the Sparks song that transcends the flatness of usual pop music.

RON MAEL IS A unique songwriter and often challenges his songwriting abilities by refusing to repeat himself. "Fletcher Honorama" has a minimal melody that builds into a dreamy landscape. Sort of sinister overtones mixed with a wishful melody. One hears the Musical Theater at work without the stage settings. Naked interpretations that you, the listener, will fill in with your imagination. All the songs have a bigger than life, almost otherworldly quality to them. "Simple Ballet" is a song that could have been written for *The Sound of Music*. One doesn't get a feeling of urban living or a sense of neighborhood in any of the songs. They're in some imaginary park or the backyard of an unspecific house or on the top of a hill looking over the city landscape. Sparks is more interested in their head as a location rather than, say, Asbury Park, NJ. There is nothing false about Sparks, though the brothers world can be slightly dangerous and phobia-inducing. Sparks takes you through this world, showing these sometimes troubling vistas, but still acting as a guide, keeping listeners safe as they look out on this world.

RUSSELL'S CONCENTRATION AND HIS ability to convey old lyrics go beyond the past and into a present that is not sure about itself. Sparks is never part of an era anyway. It is either ahead of everyone else or slightly behind. The band has its own inner clock and only acknowledges that private sense of time.

I HAVE SEEN SPARKS many times throughout its various eras, but now the band has to nail its entire history in twenty-one nights. I feel a little insane that I fell for this concept, because here I am in London with no money, and without a doubt causing the nice banker at my local Silver Lake bank a rather tremendous amount of consternation. On one level it's a major financial risk to be away from my work for this long, but on a bigger level I feel at home, where I know exactly what will happen in the theater. In many ways this is my version of a cruise on a ship where you pretty much know what your time is going to entail, while at the same time knowing that you're going to have some kind of experience.

GOING TO A SPARKS show is like going to a meeting of the Freemasons. You don't know the others in the audience, but you are there to worship, to appreciate, and to take in what is taking place on the stage—and it's an almost religious relationship within the audience. So it may be strange for that "date" to see how her boyfriend or girlfriend are really like in that private small world. Because life outside Sparks is a world not of our choosing. But in most cases, and if the person is cool, and the stars are aligned, the shows work like a miracle to the virgin.

AS AN ENCORE THEY performed "England," which is a B side from *Indiscreet*-era Sparks. An appropriate choice for their first show with respect to this series in London.

I've just come back from England
With some astounding, scientific sort of news
There exist in England living creatures
Much the same as me and you.

Sure it sounds fantastic though,
But facts are facts most everywhere
That was in New York, it was in Paris, maybe the
coast of Peru
No no no, no not fair, it was England
Yes it was, it was England
Yes it was, it was in her coal

A WOOFER IN TWEETER'S CLOTHING (1973)
MAY 17, 2008
ENCORE: "ARTS 4 CRAFTS SPECTACULAR"

Still high from the first show I have a great conversation with my dear friend Rosa and her six-year-old son, Oscar, who I am staying with for the first two weeks in London. She wants all the details from the show, like what the band was wearing and what the audience was like. The audience was the same generation as *Halfnelson's* 1972 release. No young people at all except for the few offspring who were being dragged by their parents, clearly wanting to share a passion with their children.

I have to admit there is something beautiful about bringing your kid to a show. My dad took me to see rock and roll shows numerous times, and it was always fun for me. Particularly now, when I look back on the bands that I saw and the time period that I saw them, I feel pretty lucky.

MY DAD TOOK ME to see a double bill of The Doors with Them, featuring Van Morrison. I think the purpose of our visit was to see Van sing "Gloria," but pre-first album Jim Morrison and Company weren't bad for the eyes or ears either. It was at the legendary Whisky A Go-Go in 1966, and the club started to have "kiddie matinees" to allow the under-eighteen crowd to see shows. The thing is, the sets happened around two in the afternoon. Very un-rock and roll hour. Still, I have memories of drinking Coca-Cola with a straw from a long cocktail glass and looking up at the stage and seeing Jim with the iconic leather pants performing Kurt Weill/Bertolt Brecht's "Alabama Song." What was there not to like? I was raised with "Alabama Song" sung by Lotte Leyna, and here was a new variation of the song, spoken to my specific generation. How could I consider myself anything but lucky? On top of that I got to see the other Morrison, Van, doing my favorite Them songs, "Gloria,"

"Mystic Eyes," and "Here Comes The Night." It wasn't the perfect rock and roll evening, but nevertheless probably the best rock and roll afternoon ever!

My dad also took me to see the Jimi Hendrix Experience with the Soft Machine, Electric Flag, and Blue Cheer opening for the guitar god. And yes, Hendrix was the guitar god, but Blue Cheer impressed me without playing a note, just by seeing their endless stacks of Marshall amps on the stage. I was in the fifth row at the Shrine Auditorium and looking up at the stage, seeing the sight of these black amplifiers one after the other stacked up really high. And the only song I can remember is their one hit at the time (now officially a cult band, everything they do is studied and learned), "Summertime Blues," a cover of the original masterpiece by the great Eddie Cochran. What came out when they hit the first note from that song was static noise from these stacked Marshall amps. I had never heard anything that loud, and/or seen a stack of amps that big, shaking from the volume and what seemed to be the ultimate power chord. I can't always remember the sound, but the vision of the Blue Cheer spectacle has never left me.

I also saw David Bowie's Ziggy Stardust at the Santa Monica Civic Auditorium, New York Dolls at the Hollywood Palladium, and Jobriath at the Troubadour; all of them iconic shows and all of them spent with either my dad or both parents. I didn't think about it at the time but now realize that I shared great music moments with my parents, and now I treasure that time as something special. I wished that I was sharing the Sparks in London with my dad, but death takes no reservations or rain checks.

AT THE HIGHGATE LIBRARY, I listen to "Girl From Germany," the first track on Sparks' second album, *A Woofer In A Tweeter's Clothing*. The very melody reminds me of a fellow hard worker, Charlie Chaplin, dancing with a pair of shoes on the table inside what is a snowed-in cabin in his film *The Gold Rush*.

It is around this second album that Ron developed his pre-WWII mustached look. Ron Mael's appearance has the Chaplin charm with the Hitler darkness. It is specifically these two iconic figures that Ron deals with. One is taboo and evil incarnated. The other, one of the greatest comedians that ever lived. But even comedians have some darker moments; in *The*

Great Dictator Chaplin portrays Hitler as a near future menace, although one also wonders if Chaplin identifies with Hitler not only in a visual sense, but also in recognizing the evil within humanity that eventually will destroy and poison the landscape. Hitler is the absence of hope and Chaplin personifies hope. A duality that is in constant tension within the music of Sparks.

Hitler didn't come out of the pure blue sky. Somewhere within that post-WWII culture, a monster was allowed to germinate from a wounded soldier and failed artist to a racist tyrant. Chaplin saw that trajectory and commented on it. Weirdly enough both men were born the same year and only four days apart. I wonder if Chaplin thought about his character, the Tramp, in relation to Hitler? The dictator, I presume, felt that he was meant to be on a higher plane than the rest of the German citizenry. Chaplin, on the other hand, wanted to share a gift with humanity, to make people laugh.

Charlie Chaplin, when wearing the costume of Hitler (or his character Adenoid Hynkel), he was reported to be very aggressive and difficult to work with. Chaplin, I think, was aware that he had that seed of craziness in himself—his mom was reported to have suffered from syphilis to have been insane.

Ron and Russell, brothers, play out these identities of good and evil through their music and onstage. They play with meanings through both their music and their aesthetic.

British song and dance man, Tommy Handley (who, along with my dad, was a face on the Beatles' *Sgt. Pepper's Lonely Hearts Club Band* album cover) wrote a song called "Who Is That Man? (Who Looks Like Charlie Chaplin)" about the Chaplin and Hitler identity.

Now we've seen a lot of pictures of the people in the news, and we've
got to know a lot of them, by sight.
Chamberlain, with his umbrella Winston Churchill
with his hats
Or Belitia, well we know him, all right
But there's one who's lovely photograph we've seen
for years and
years
And we ask ourselves this question every time his
face appears...
Who is this man who looks like Charlie Chaplin?
What makes him think that he can win a war?
It can't be the mustache...that only makes us laugh
And Charlie's done it better...and before.
If it wasn't for the boots and cane and trousers,

You couldn't tell the two of them apart
But the whole idea's absurd
Charlie's never said a word
And Adolf couldn't play a silent part
Imagine Adolf starring in "The Gold Rush'
He hasn't got a half of Charlie's charms
But he gives a lot of troubles ... to his film director,
Goebbels
When he plays the leading part in 'Shoulder Arms'
He's amusing when he tries to play the villain
It's bound to get a laugh in every clime
I believe it's all a fake-up
And despite all of the make-up
We're convinced it's Charlie Chaplin...all the time.
Supposing Charlie Chaplin got the fever
A war would be a comedy pro tem
Imagine Adolf getting skittish...signing pacts with
'Gaumont British'
And dropping custard pies on 'MGM'
Charlie Chaplin would be louder, bigger, funnier
With him in charge the battles would be fun
And the chief of his gestapo wouldn't be Karl
Marx...but Harpo
And he's soon have Shirley Temple on the run
If Adolf was in business, he'd try sob-stuff
East Lym would be the story from the start
Little Eva, played by Goring would be trifle boring

I'd sooner see Charles Laughton in the part
But don't let us be too hard on poor old Adolf
He's a godsend to the comics, he's sublime
Cartoonists love his make-up...but one morning we
shall wake up
And find it's Charlie Chaplin all the time!

AS FAR AS I know Ron Mael has had the Chaplin/ Hitler mustache since the *A Woofer In Tweeter's Clothing* album came out, but the look became crystal clear on the *Kimono My House* album cover.

The real surprise of this evening's set was how powerful the songs "Beaver O'Lindy," "Nothing is Sacred," and "Moon Over Kentucky" were. Russell's voice soared like the inner-twenty-year-old that he truly is. I imagine if Bertolt Brecht had a contemporary rock band this would be the group. One cannot help but be reminded of the connection between "Moon Over Kentucky" and Weill and Brecht's "Moon Over Alabama" from the fantastic and influential *The Threepenny Opera*.

The Weill/Brecht influence resonates not only in its melodies, but also in its themes and aesthetic. The melodies are rich and incredibly tuneful, but the complex time changes in the song challenge the listener.

Furthering the Weill/Brecht connection, Sparks played two songs thematically revolving around WWII: "Do-Re-Mi" from *The Sound of Music*, which sounds as though Sparks could have written it, and "Girl From Germany," which Sparks did write. Both hint at the menace of the times, but never dwell on its horror, choosing instead to hint at the horror on its way around the corner.

"Girl From Germany" revolves around a son who brings his German girlfriend home to meet his parents, who are freaked out because they can't forget the war. The album is mostly about the aftereffects of a terrible, yet vague event that occurred somewhere in the past.

THE A WOOFER IN *Tweeter's Clothing* concert is incredibly passionate, the band members were on fire. They were tight, full of expression, and brought this album a new life. The recording of *Woofer* is very flat sounding, but live interpretation is like watching a new preservation print of a D. W. Griffith classic. The images become clearer, sharper, and the songs live outside of the vinyl disc. Sparks didn't do these shows as a nostalgic journey to the past, but to make a statement on its role in contemporary pop music history.

THEIR ENCORE, "ARTS & Crafts Spectacular," is an unreleased Sparks song from sometime between the first and second albums. Lost and forgotten until Morrissey put it on a collection of his favorite songs, *Under The Influence*. My guess is that Sparks hadn't heard this song for years 'til Morrissey brought it out again. No one really knows how he even got a hold of this recording but it's now considered an essential Sparks track.

I WALK OUT OF Carling Academy into the cool Islington night and think about the area I am inhabiting for twenty-one nights. It was referenced in Charles Dickens' *Oliver Twist*: *"The couch rattled away and, turning when it reached the Angel at Islington, stopped at length before a neat house in Pentonville."* And there is a possibility that Thomas Paine wrote sections of *Rights of Man* at the Old Red Lion located near St. John Street.

NEARBY PENTONVILLE PRISON IS the famous home for the prisoners Oscar Wilde and Pete Doherty. The last hanging at Pentonville took place in 1961. The gentleman's name was Edwin Bush. He came up from a rough family situation where two adults and six children lived in a three-room home. At the age of twenty-one, he killed Elsie May Batten, the wife of Mark Batten, the president of the Royal Society of British Sculptors.

COINCIDENTALLY, AND SOMEWHAT DISTURBINGLY, a young man was knifed in the stomach outside the Academy tonight, during the show. I don't know if he survived.

KIMONO MY HOUSE (1974)
MAY 18, 2008
ENCORE: "BARBECUTIE"

Out of all of the albums of music ever recorded, if I had to pick just one as my favorite, it would be *Kimono My House*. I picked it up because of the photograph of Ron and Russell on the back cover of the album. Specifically Ron's look, which was almost unhealthily thin, wearing a pullover sweater, baggy pants, dark tie, and the Hitler/Chaplin mustache.

Aesthetic icons can be made within seconds, and it struck me immediately. I was looking for a band that expressed my desire for radical change from the past, a band that broke from rock traditions that seemed tired and out of touch to me.

Teenagers in the fifties had Elvis; Sparks was *my* Elvis. I loved them because they seemed to be a band that said no to rock, yet rocked harder than anyone. It was rock for people who had trouble of thinking of rock as a way of life. People like me who needed rock, but couldn't deal with the trappings of rock culture, which seemed constantly to lead to a dead end. What was once a music force became a pledge to misery. Ron's dandyish distain of things around him had a profound effect on me. As though at last Noël Coward came back to life and spoke through Ron.

AT ONE POINT THERE were plans to make a Sparks film called *Confusion* with the great French film-maker and comedian Jacques Tati, whose dark soul soaks through his films like fingerprints on a murder weapon. Tati is unique amongst mid-twentieth century filmmakers. A silent artist, he used sound in a way no one had ever heard before, much in the same way that Sparks used visual media with their music in a way that bands had never done before. In both instances, the visual and aural don't mesh in a traditional sense. Their juxtaposition helps to reveal new meaning in the audio and the visual. Sparks is almost cinematic in its appearance, and Tati is musical in his filmic direction. They were a match made in heaven.

For his film *Playtime*, Tati built a whole fake city, a completely artificial world that was both aesthetically pleasing and endlessly frightening. Similarly, the beauty of Sparks' melodies often contrast the ugliness of the world described within the lyrics. What lies in the landscape is an emotional minefield.

Spanning multiple genres over the bands career, Sparks quickly passed out of rock and into various other types of music. *Kimono My House* has tango as well as some waltz rhythms. *Kimono* is like South America filtered through glam rock in some rundown theater in Vienna, with a dab of light operetta. "Fall In Love With Myself Again" is surely a young Ron before he met up with himself thirty-some years later with "I Married Myself" (from *Lil' Beethoven*).

ICONIC TO THE CORE, but unable to be repeated, *Kimono My House* is a combination of pure spiritual misery, bliss, and dark humor. It takes chances that pop music wouldn't normally take. Still, this album and its singles (particularly "This Town Ain't Big Enough For The Both Of Us") became a hit in the U.K. in 1974.

SEEING THEM PERFORM KIMONO My House is not as unique an experience as last night's show; the album is a classic, even among those who are not hardcore Sparks fanatics. For many, including me, it was the first Sparks album we were introduced to.

The live show of Kimono is like being thrown in ice-cold water after a feverish night in bed. The music on the album is paced in a frantic manner with no ballads whatsoever. There are a plethora of beautiful melodies, however, with unrelenting galloping rhythms. It's relentless and in a certain way reminds me of the Ramones' first album, in that the music and lyrics are consistently in your face. By no means is this background or wallpaper music. It demands to be heard and doesn't take any prisoners.

Kimono is one of the sold out shows at the Islington Carling Academy. Which, of course, is not a surprise. This is also not a rare album; Sparks did a live version for Morrissey's Meltdown Festival in London not long ago. Kimono is a sentimental favorite for many in the audience. And for people like me, who listened to Kimono alone in their bedroom, it had a radical effect on our personalities.

This album is so special to me—almost like my DNA is mixed in the vinyl grooves. It is also the one album that made those who never heard of Sparks suddenly became aware of the band's oddness. Sparks represented the nerds who thought too much.

Since I was in America at the time of *Kimono's* release, and was probably one of the few in the United States that actually owned this album when it was released in that foreign world known as London, I always felt as though the album held some kind of special power. Like the One Ring, I had something that no one else possessed. I felt powerful with *Kimono*, like I could escape to my room and then to swinging London by putting that needle into the groove of the album.

To be at this concert for this specific album, with these fans was like drinking a fine red wine. When the album came out, I felt so separate from the British audience that picked up on *Kimono*; to be here on English soil to see and hear the album that majorly shifted in a large group of British listeners was simply amazing.

THERE IS A PART of me that loathes being a part of any community, though. Since *Kimono* is an iconic piece of work, the community expands exponentially at the Carling Academy on this night. The problem is that the show doesn't have anything new for *me*. The performance is great, but it doesn't hold any surprises. It is a perfect live reproduction of a perfect album with an audience around my age, and thus should be the ultimate evening. But for whatever reason I find myself wanting more.

ONE OF THE THINGS that impressed me when I first purchased *Kimono My House* was the absence of a title or band name on the front cover, only a humorous portrait of two Japanese girls wearing formal kimonos. Without the title on the front, I had to really pay attention to the cover before I turned it around to figure out who even created this album and what it was called.

When I finally put the album on my record player that over-the-top glam sound that is almost Orson Wellesian in its scope blared through the speakers. It reminded of the last scene in *Citizen Kane* where the camera pulls back to expose the giant room full of material possessions, a life wasted, but well spent, literally.

There are only a handful of recordings that make me feel like I am in a new world: Roxy Music and the Ramones' first few albums and *Kimono My House*. Every one of those albums, sounded like they came from another planet. To this day, these recordings are as fresh as the thoughts behind them. They're radical works that borrow from the past to make a new future.

Kimono My House is like a Kabuki play, very flat where all the action happens in one view, the complexity lying in its simplicity. You have to take the whole picture and not separate it into various parts. When I first heard this album I sat down thinking that this is my life on vinyl. And thirty-four years later, I still feel that this album could be my emotional biography.

UNLIKE A WOOFER IN *Tweeter's Clothing*, I have spent so much time listening to this album that the live show is anticlimactic. Though sonically beautiful, and visually interesting, as all Sparks shows tend to be, there wasn't much new for me to hear. Maybe because I have seen Sparks so many times, and heard these songs so many times, but this live show didn't awaken me to new meanings in the music as last night's show did. To give credit, *Woofer* had nowhere to go but up, and *Kimono* couldn't be in much better standing. Still, as I leave Carling Academy I felt sort of sad and at the same time hopeful for what tomorrow night will bring.

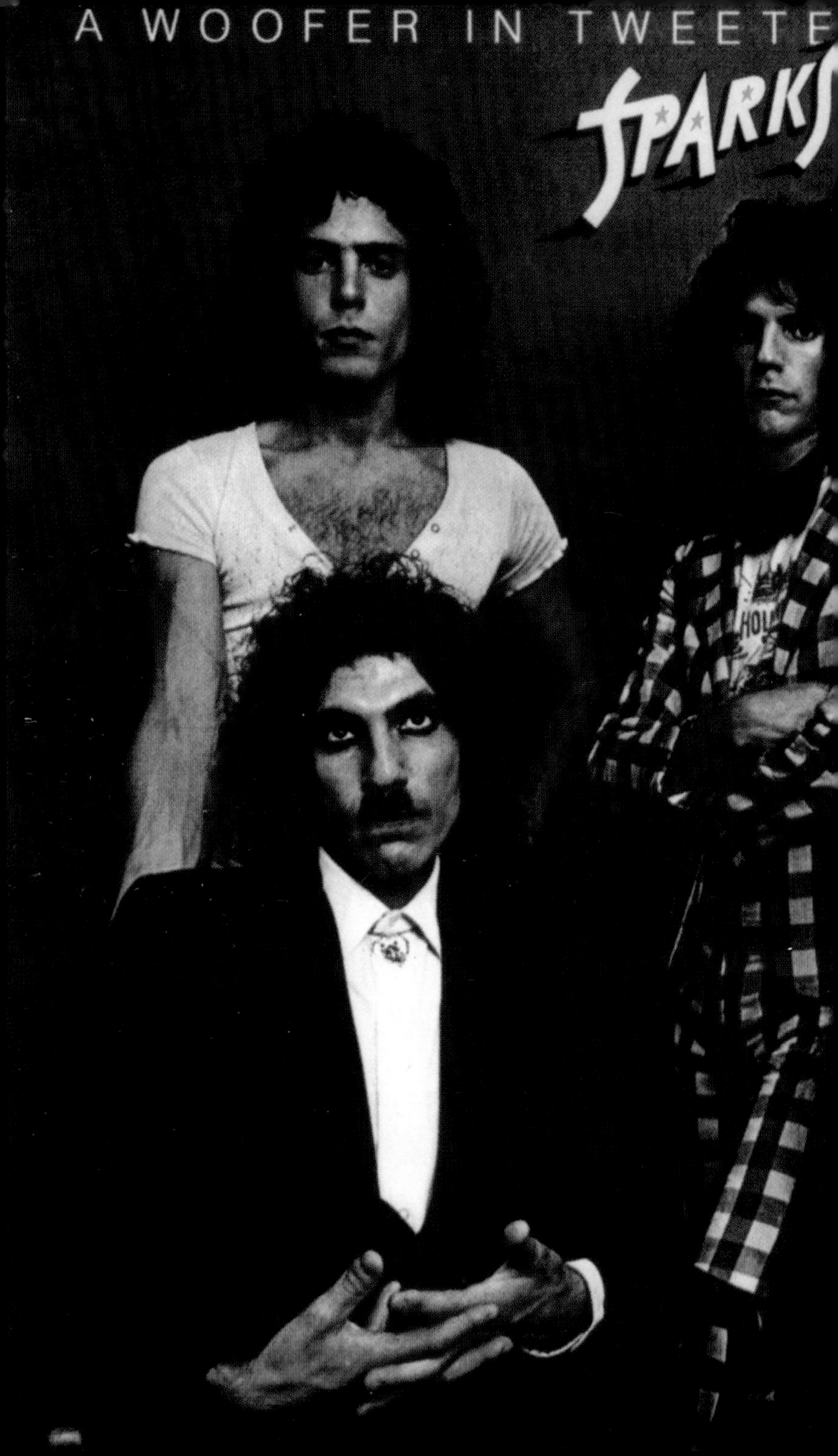
A WOOFER IN TWEETE
SPARKS

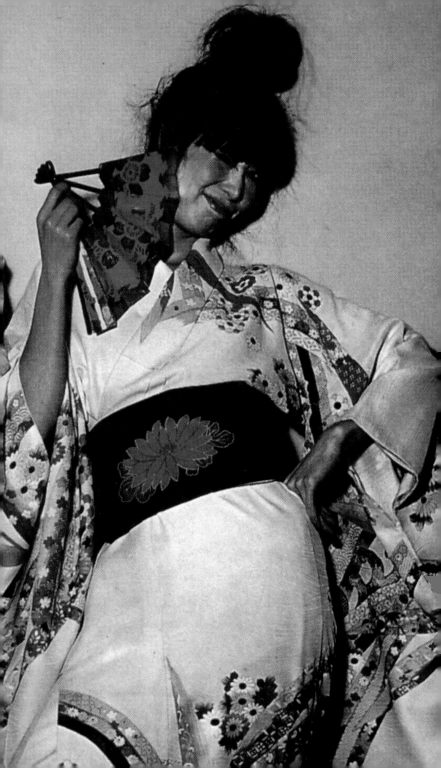

SPARKS/INDISCREET

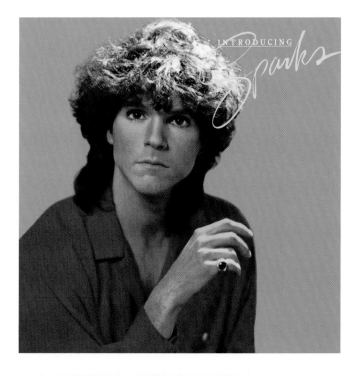

Sparks.
Terminal Jive.

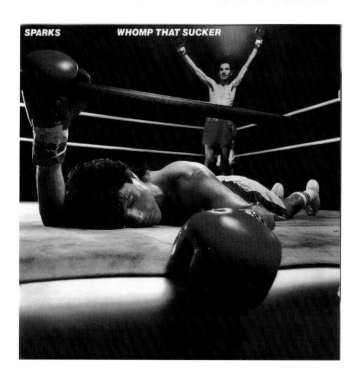

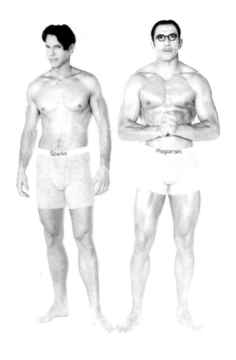

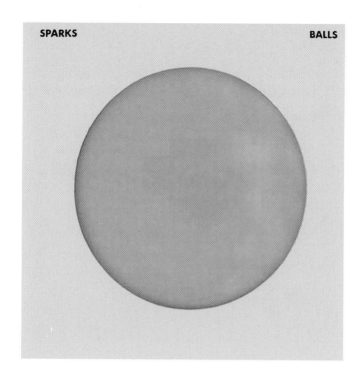

Lil' Beethoven

An Album By
S P A R K S

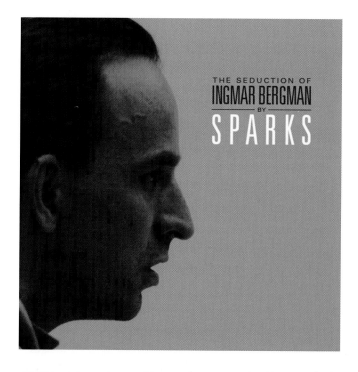

PROPAGANDA (1974)
MAY 28, 2008
ENCORE: "LOST AND FOUND"

Propaganda proved to the world that Sparks' first three albums had not been a lucky streak by a lunatic songwriter in a Hitler/ Chaplin mustache. The songs just got better and the production flourishes by producer Muff Winwood—who started working with Sparks on *Kimono My House*—just kept getting tighter. The all-English backup band played like they had torches under them, intensifying the already busy arrangement of the songs in *Propaganda*. The record was more artificial than their previous albums. It was a world made by Sparks for Sparks.

PROPAGANDA IS A WAR album, an album of WWI to be specific. In the first song, "Reinforcements," war is superimposed over a relationship between boy and girl.

Kimono is a lot of little brush strokes capturing a single incident, a single feeling, but Propaganda is a cast of thousands, covering similar issues as Kimono with deeper and grander emotions. If Kimono My House was a play, it would be a Brecht production in a rundown small theater somewhere in East Berlin, while Propaganda would be a Broadway musical.

THE MOST MOVING AND romantic ballad on this album is "Bon Voyage." It's about watching death from a distance. The song is about the sinking of an ocean liner, with the singer saying goodbye to all the people who are stranded and about to go down with the ship. This is a classic Sparks motif. On one level it sort of says, "Sorry, pal," but it is simultaneously a beautiful meditation on the nature of death and why some must go and others survive. The lyrics are funny, yet moving:

> "Saunter up the gangway/The randomest sampling is complete/God, could there be some way/That I could/wear a hood/or by the/way I stood/Sneak aboard with you."

RUSSELL SINGS THIS SONG without a trace of irony. There is something very haunting about the image of someone watching the ship go down, and knowing it is either by luck or design that they are not the one on the ship. The viewer of this tragedy, can't help but be happy, while the humanity of watching this ship sink and being unable to help is devastating.

The entire album, *Propaganda,* is rich in the texture of the narrative matched with the melodies. I am looking forward to the live version of this album to see how they will convey the delicate balance between its harsh humor and the beauty of the songs. I wonder how they will do it live and if it will have the same bite that it does on vinyl.

FOR THE FIRST SHOW, the *Halfnelson* show, the audience was pretty old, and by old I mean my age and a little older. But with each subsequent show, the audiences' age bracket is expanding to include younger and younger fans.

Propaganda is up there with the second album in its intensity and the band is just raring into the songs with such abandonment and joy. Steve McDonald, the bass player (of Redd Kross), is for some reason always the one who I can see clearly from the audience. He looks like a kid who discovered the key to the candy store. It's nice to know that the band, along with the audience members, is feeling the same way about this special event. There's a sense of camaraderie amongst all of us in Carling Academy. We're all in this together.

When I'm in the audience I refuse to be anywhere but on the floor in front of the stage, right in the middle. I can feel the intensity of the audience in the back and in front of me, and I try to look at the faces in the crowd. I try to read their expressions and thoughts of being here in this exact moment. There are no casual concertgoers here, no one just thought it would be nice to see a Sparks show and bought a ticket on a whim. We are all a part of the cult, the club, and we all ascribe to the vision of Sparks. Because Sparks rarely plays in public, a Sparks show is an intense experience, like having sex with that one person you've always wanted, and then never seeing her or him again. And this, being at the beginning of this series of shows, is even more intense than the other Sparks shows I've been lucky enough to see. This is like having a one night stand with Casanova.

I would rather be on the floor than backstage or upstairs in the VIP section, but even when I visit the VIP section, every single person is singing along with an intense passion. I imagine it is a musician's fantasy to hold an audience so captivated that they can't even look away. I often ask Russell if he can feel the audience from the stage. He can. He basks in the beauty of being onstage and watching the fans as they let Sparks songs wash over them in the darkness of the theater.

Smelling the farts, the drunken breath, the sex, the ickyness of being closed in with our fellow Sparks fans is all part of the concert experience. I wouldn't trade it for anything.

EARLIER THIS AFTERNOON I went to Borders Islington (directly across from Carling Academy) for the Mael brothers' signing of their new album *Exotic Creatures of the Deep*. It was sold out. I didn't know a signing could be sold out. I thought sold out could only happen at a signing if they ran out of things to sell. Apparently the tickets were limited to 150, and I didn't have a ticket. I really didn't want one, I just wanted to watch the procedure and how they dealt with the meet and greet. So I just hung out in the store to assess what was happening. For a chain store, this Borders wasn't bad. They had my favorite author, Patrick Hamilton, on the shelves, and played *Kimono My House* instead of the new album. Classy move.

THE TRIP AT THIS point has been a solitary one. I left my wife back home and it has been difficult to work here without seeing her every morning. We tend to work in different parts of the house, but the thought that she is just around the corner from my writing spot is a sense of security for me. It's weird that she's not here. On the upside I am staying with our friend Rosa and her beautifully unique and brilliant six-year-old son Oscar. Oscar hates it when I leave the house without him, and it's kind of nice that someone notices me when I am not around. Oscar wants to be a dress designer, and at six he has a notebook full of ideas and drawings. All women's clothing and out there designs make me wonder if he will be a Sparks fan like me in the future?

Oscar's mom is from Tokyo, and an exquisite beauty. Doll-like in nature, yet strong-willed, she is the perfect drinking companion when I get back from the shows. Most of the time she is asleep with Oscar, which makes me think of ways to wake her so she can have a bottle of wine with me. I refrain, however. The nights when she is up, it is a real treat.

I FIRST MET ROSA when I first met my wife. They were partners in crime: Lun*na did her clothing/costumes and Rosa performed onstage. It was performance art that bordered on a combination of English variety stage show and Japanese Vaudeville. Rosa is currently focusing on photography as her medium of expression, and the images she makes are quite startling and fantastic. She reminds me of Cindy Sherman, but Rosa's work has more soul—maybe because the images are not based on a false identity, like Sherman's, but instead based on Rosa's personality. She used to do a series of self-portraits but now focuses on her son with a series of portraits that make Oscar look like a child from the turn of the century England. Page boy haircut, handmade clothing, mainly little girls blouses—he's a gender-bending child on one level while being a typical little boy on another.

AS A HOSTESS, ROSA treats me better than I could have ever expected. She puts up with all my stupid questions about London culture, while giving me complicated instructions on how to get from one location to another in this great capital. Incredible patience, amazing grace, to say I am a fan of hers is to put it mildly. I took her and Oscar out to lunch for her birthday a few days ago, at a Thai restaurant somewhere in Kentish Town. I haven't really sat down and had a meal with anyone since I got to Europe. It was nice.

INDISCREET (1975)
MAY 21, 2008
ENCORE: "GONE WITH THE WIND"

Before the *Indiscreet* show started, I went to the Camden Arts Centre in North London to meet Bruce Haines, one of the curators at the city-owned museum. They're going to do a Wallace Berman solo exhibition, so I spent the day there locating certain art pieces by my dad. Being a curator is similar to being a detective, they look for the facts and names behind artwork, and what the timeline was after it was introduced to the world.

I FIND THERE IS a slight depression associated with encountering my past like this, like I am constantly being pulled back further and further. And even though it is difficult for me, I feel I owe it to my dad and his work to help with things like this, to describe the stories that I remember and have heard about his works of art. An afternoon of going through my father's artwork, how the pieces were done and what happened to them afterward, left me with a heavy heart.

I THEN THOUGHT OF what these twenty-one nights must mean to Ron and Russell. To spend four months rehearsing the songs in Los Angeles before coming to London, and rehearsing every day while they are here. It must bring back memories, both good and bad. No album is made without some kind of emotional catalyst, and I'm sure they have memories of each and every one of the twenty-one albums. Between memorizing the songs that are long forgotten, focusing on the arrangements, and finding songs not on albums that they could use for an encore performance every night, the effort put into this is monumental. Like Bruce Haines doing curatorial work at the Camden Arts Centre for my dad's exhibition, Sparks too is curating a lifetime of work in sizable bites.

Putting together a show by an artist like my father with a rather long career is overwhelming. Showing where he came from and where he went, takes dedication and love. Ron and Russell, without an outside curator taking charge, are going through their closets and hiding places to put together this simply awesome series of concerts. I find myself wondering if they look at it as a piece of history or a living work of art.

EVEN AT THE TIME I bought the album, *Indiscreet* felt like a passageway that would be closed once entered. Like Alice falling into the rabbit hole, I would be changed forever, and I suspect that for Sparks, making this album was a huge turning point. Legendary producer Tony Visconti helped Sparks push the boundaries, dabbling in all sorts of different genres in this album. Flitting from big band to rock, and even hinting at a new wave sound at certain points, *Indiscreet* marks another new beginning.

Because of the nature of the arrangements, I wasn't sure what to expect from this show. Of all the shows so far, this is the one I was looking forward to the most. Would they stay with the original arrangements? And if so, how? At least three or four of the songs have very particular string arrangements as well as a brass section.

Lyrically, it varies greatly from the other albums, referring to things that are outside the Sparks world. It has an American cultural history feel to it, sometimes it even feels Aaron Copelandesque, expressing a big land with big musical gestures. *Propaganda* has a similar gesture to American music, but on a narrow canvas, and *Indiscreet* throws a net over a bigger version of American culture. It makes me think of a giant American musical—something classic like *Oklahoma*, *Annie Get Your Gun*, or of that ilk from Broadway's Golden Age.

With Tony Visconti at the helm, the songs seem larger than your run-of-the-mill pop tunes. It's almost as though a chorus of dancers are tapping to the album above an orchestra pit. Visconti produced the key David Bowie albums, as well as the classic T. Rex records, and seems to have had the key to the studio as well as the budget it would take to make Sparks' vision of *Indiscreet* into a Technicolor classic *aural* film.

Not surprisingly, the performance of *Indiscreet* was superb. They brought in a string section as well as a brass section for "Get in the Swing." I don't believe Sparks has ever performed this song onstage and they certainly have never done "Without Using Hands" or "Under the Table With Her." They're beautifully crafted baroque pop songs, delicate yet breakable like priceless china on an unstable surface.

Indiscreet was the last of the adventurous variety Sparks album. After this the band went off in other directions, exploring the outside world, instead of looking in on the world of Sparks.

Indiscreet is a variety show that goes from sped up contemporary pop to fiddles of the late twenties. Whenever I hear Visconti's production in this album, I think of floor floodlights on the stage with Russell in a checkered suit. Is that the actual reality of the live show? No, not really.

IT WAS WHILE I was watching this show that I realized I too have a duality. I feel I am performing under the name of "Tosh" and that figure is a fictional character. Because of the business I'm in, that of selling books, I have a different public persona than my private one. Maybe it has something to do with being the executor of my dad's estate, but I am often asked to be representative of an artist that is no longer able to represent his own work. In my normal life,

I really don't have a lot to say aloud, and am instead compelled to write.

This show speaks to my blood, guts, and brain, it speaks to my soul, recognizing that every person lives multiple lives within their singular life. Speaking to the fact that we all live in plurality, that we all in our own ways put on many masks. And at the end of the show, it's time for me to leave my writer's mask and slip on the friend mask that I wear at Rosa's house.

BIG BEAT (1976)
MAY 23, 2008
ENCORE "TEARING THE PLACE APART"

1976 was not a good year for me. My father, who bought the album *Propaganda* for me, died in a car accident. He was killed by a drunk driver in Topanga Canyon. Everything changed in my world the moment he died. It was like he dragged my entire world to the grave with him.

To this day it strikes me as weird that someone who I spent every day with for the first twenty-one years of my life is gone permanently. It is a loss that I still have trouble wrapping my head around. Almost every night I have a dream that features my father, not the same dream, but he is always there somewhere, even if he's just in the background. In many ways he didn't die, he stays with me always. I have no recollection of crying over my dad's death, except in a dream, many years after his death; I realized in that dream that he was dead. In all my other dreams he is very much alive and with me. There is a big part of me that, even after all these years, refuses to accept his passing at all. I know it happened, but it seems like it happened in someone else's movie.

In 1976, I BECAME even more obsessed with Sparks while simultaneously falling in love with punk. The British Invasion hit me hard as a child, but the punk scene was something that as an adult I grasped with a mixture of pleasure and disgust. After my father's death, I felt as though I had to start my life over again. Punk gave me the liberty to do just that.

I LOVED THE THOUGHT of a movement that wanted to destroy the past in order to move forward. Punk was into the destruction of bands that I loved in the sixties, and a part of me needed that, needed to destroy my past in a certain way. I bought the whole punk movement without second-guessing it, without really thinking through what exactly it meant to destroy the past.

I was going through a period of despair—maybe I still am—and that whole year just consisted of me floundering in my doubt and depression. *Taxi Driver* was released that year and I saw that film in a theater at least twenty-five times. At the time I couldn't imagine seeing any other film except *Taxi Driver*. Whenever anyone asked me to go to a movie, I always insisted on seeing *Taxi Driver* again. I didn't identify with the Robert De Niro character, but I wanted to experience the film's sadness over and over again. It made my sadness more manageable for some reason. I wore my unhappiness like a winter coat. I embraced it and fed the misery with my thoughts, heart, and by seeing *Taxi Driver* numerous times. Sparks released an album that year, an album that sounded one hundred percent different from their other releases.

Sparks has always been there, in my darkest piss hole to my brightest days. My mood swings always allowed the world of Sparks to enter the private residence that is otherwise known as my head. Sadly and interesting enough 1976 and *Big Beat* were the beginning of a very dark period for me and Sparks.

The year punk broke out Sparks went back to the electric guitar and left the grand orchestrations behind. When I first heard *Big Beat*, I thought, *where's Ron?* The arrangements were more straightforward, and the songs were more matter-of-fact.

After the adventurous first five albums, *Big Beat* struck me as a conservative record by a never-conservative duo. Here they were making music in tune with the times, instead of ignoring everything that was happening culturally, as they had for the first albums. Overall, I think the album suffers from its attempt at conforming to the new wave and punk scenes. The irony is that Sparks is more punk, artistically speaking, than anything else out there.

Big Beat is not my favorite Sparks album. In retrospect, however, it may be one of the most interesting pieces that the band has ever released, because of its moody aura and, in some parts of the album, its hints at evil that are so out of character compared to earlier works.

"Throw Her Away (And Get A New One)" is a nasty piece of work. Sparks is not known for its romantic sentiments, but this song has a stinging bitterness. It's the only Sparks song that I have moral issues with, and I'm not really moralistic.

It is a record about a world that crumbled, whereas earlier albums dealt with a world *about to* crumble. Here we see the total destruction of the soul, and what was once male indifference is now nasty and hostile.

Big Beat is a short yet humorously brutal album that I find truly troubling. It's not just the nature of womanhood being critiqued and attacked, but also this is the only album of theirs that comments on a specific gender while being thuggish. The more I look into this album the more disturbing the images are that come from some deep dark place. It's humorous, yes, but one tastes the bitterness coming through the vinyl.

It's like the world that was built up on *Indiscreet* has been torn apart and ravaged—and the ones who are left alive are facing these demons. *Big Beat* came out when I was facing some of my biggest demons, and I will always be thankful for the fact that Sparks gave me an album that reminded me I wasn't the only one with tragedy. My father's death had changed me profoundly. In a sense, it was a new Tosh listening to Sparks.

THE ONE REALLY INTERESTING song on *Big Beat* that could have been a fantastic project is "Confusion," which was going to be the Jacques Tati film. Tati wanted to do a film about a television studio where Russell was the director and Ron played the camera operator. This song is the only piece that exists that is attached to the doomed project, which was put on indefinite hold due to Tati's death.

BECAUSE THIS ALBUM CAME out the year my father died, I have been looking forward to hearing *this album* live, or rather I have been anticipating hearing this album live, sort of like revisiting the scene of the crime in order to assess the damage and judge how much I've recovered from it.

TONIGHT'S PERFORMANCE OF BIG *Beat* is in-your-face great. In a way, it was a great reality check for me. As much as it sometimes seems that I'll never move forward from my dad's death, nights like this remind me that I have. That I live my life with my father's memory with me, but am not being held back by the tragedy of his death.

Sparks' encore for the evening is one of the band's great songs about loss, kind of a final nod to my own feelings and struggles. As usual, Sparks give me the emotional shot in the arm that I need exactly when I need it. "Tearing the

Place Apart" is about a man noticing the objects that are leaving his home because of a breakup. I always identified with this song because of a bad breakup I had with a serious girlfriend, her leaving didn't affect me as much as her taking objects that she owned or we shared, which tore me apart.

Big Beat, done live, takes on a theatrical bent. The spectacle of it all is missing on the recordings and the material sounds flat and one dimensional, even on vinyl, but live it is a different beast. Like *Indiscreet,* Russell takes a role onstage; I think I missed the wink-wink to the listeners of the recordings that I see here at the live show. It's a dark album that smells of America going to pot in its grooves. *Big Beat* is a combination of what was out there in 1976, disappointments waiting for the Sex Pistols, after which there is no turning back. As one can see on the next album...

INTRODUCING SPARKS (1977)
MAY 24, 2008
ENCORE: "ALABAMY RIGHT"

After the bleakness of *Big Beat*, Sparks didn't exactly run back to their old, more European sound, instead they headed toward the more slick pop that was coming out of Los Angeles at the time. Beach Boys on their minds, innocence in their brains, and their hearts complicated by the indifference of girls, the Mael brothers hurtled toward pop music in a way they never had before. On *Introducing Sparks* they avoided the more serious issues that came up on *Big Beat* and focused on the sounds of the music, which, on this album was being performed by members of Toto.

INTRODUCING SPARKS IS ECCENTRICITY working its way through the medium of mainstream pop, which makes it sort of perverse yet enjoyable. There is a tension between the slickness of the arrangements, the crystal-clear ability of the musicians, and the sunny sound of the pop music. Live, they strip the production down but keep the backup vocals as part of the song arrangements.

WHEN I FIRST HEARD *Introducing Sparks* I didn't like it because of the slick production, which was so not 1977. That year punk broke big, and there was the feeling that anything before punk needed to be either destroyed or deemed the enemy. Slickness in record production was looked down upon. Toto was (and still is, as far as I am concerned) the enemy of progress and taste.

I remember bringing this album home to Topanga. At the time I was living with my girlfriend in the family garage. Before my father's death, he turned the garage into a swinging bachelor's den for me. Not sure why he did this, he must have presumed that I would never leave the nest. Which was pretty strange at the time, kids moved out of the house at eighteen and went to college or got a job and never went back. I, on the other hand, did nothing.

I fell in love with a woman and moved her into my bachelor's den. It was a different kind of household than most at that time. My mom had a roommate for a while, and then she had a second husband. All this time I was with this particular woman, and we shared the kitchen and bathroom with my mom. It didn't make sense, but that's Topanga for you.

The Topanga house—like the whole canyon—was haunted. Many times in the middle of the night, I would feel like I was being dragged out of my bed by a force of some sort. It felt like someone was pulling my feet into the air. Another night my girlfriend woke me up to let me know she heard a really creepy flute. I couldn't hear it, but the dogs in the neighborhood were going crazy. She hummed me the melody as it was happening and it was bone chilling.

My girlfriend was extremely beautiful, and a day didn't go by where I didn't have to fight another male's attention toward her. Being with her was hard work in the way that young relationships are. The hassle of fighting off other male attention was extremely draining and impossible to deal with after awhile. It was like she had some kind of mating call that drew men toward her at all times of the day. It was all sorts of men—professionals, doctors, musicians, married men, it just went on and on. I am not really a jealous type, but I became painfully aware that my entire purpose in life was to pay attention to her at all times or run the risk of losing her to the beasts that were howling outside the door. After a while I decided (rather, *she* decided) to end the relationship, which was, without a doubt, doomed to failure. At the time I went back to my least stressful relationship: loving Sparks' vinyl albums. *Introducing Sparks* is the seventh album, kind of tongue-in-cheek and not my favorite, but it got me through.

RECENTLY I PURCHASED THE reissue of *Introducing Sparks* and somehow my opinion of the album shifted. The songs are smooth as water and lovelier than I remembered. Why did I have a problem with it in the first place? I had thought it was too mainstream a sound at the time for Sparks. In 2008 it's a masterpiece, but in 1977 it was an embarrassment.

"Those Mysteries" is a classic ballad, a beautiful scene of questioning. Unlike *Big Beat* Sparks comes back to a world that has no bearing with the real world. *Introducing Sparks* also comes back from the black-and-white world of *Big Beat* to the colorful world that resembles Southern California.

Hearing this California-style album live in Islington creates an odd feeling of misplacement. It doesn't have an ounce of British flavor in its music, yet I found it very moving to hear this album performed live in London. It made me realize how far I had come from when I first listened to this album. Sometimes it's hard to see how far you've come in your life until you have a signpost to judge it against. In many ways, Sparks' various albums are my signposts.

RIGHT AROUND THE CORNER from the Carling Academy is Upper Street, and up that street is the Collins Music Hall. It was the first vaudeville-style theater that projected movies for an audience in the U.K. It was also the theater that showcased the talents of Charlie Chaplin right before he left for America to do movies, the Collins Music Hall helped give Islington a reputation as an arts center. It was a Mecca for writers—Charles Lamb, Charles Dickens, and George Orwell, among others—as well as for music hall entertainers. Sparks tends to straddle both worlds, with literary song lyrics and music hall-like performances, the band seems right at home in the context of Islington.

Upper Street is home to a wide array of entertainment history, the Hope & Anchor—a pub where bands like Joy Division, The Damned, and U2 have all played—was the first to have the band Madness and various other new wave and punk bands in the seventies. Islington is also home to The Screen on Green where Sid Vicious made his first appearance with the Sex Pistols on April 3, 1977.

I FEEL COMFORTED IN knowing that Chaplin performed a couple of blocks away from the Sparks venue. The roots of Ron's performances are in both Chaplin and Buster Keaton. Sparks' art must exist on a live stage as well as on the recordings because the work is so theatrical. On record the songs may be a bit more one dimensional, but the live performance takes on a different life. It refuses to see the world in a natural light. It's a kind of film that demands to be produced on a cabaret stage. So it seems a perfect fit that Sparks is doing the huge retrospective just half a mile away from Chaplin's stage.

HEARING *INTRODUCING SPARKS* PERFORMED live with the backup vocals done well, it morphs from a flat sounding record to a remarkable piece of work. Though not their best, by any means, it really swings when performed live. Night after night, Russell has not faltered in the delivery of any single song. I never get the impression that he's reciting the lyrics, he seems to relive the material and feels their meaning as he travels through them.

Russell Mael has a unique voice, but he's also an artist who knows how to express the multilevel meanings and emotions in his songs. There is absolutely nothing campy or rock and roll about him. If anything he resembles a classic salon singer during the live shows. He tackles the Sparks songs as if they were the lost classics of the American songbook.

NO. 1 IN HEAVEN (1979)
MAY 25, 2008
ENCORE: "TOO DANGEROUS TO DANCE"

The rain is going nuts this morning and I haven't even awakened from my dreams. My brain is in Los Angeles, but my body is aware it's here. I have been dreaming about Book Soup lately, and am starting to have anxiety dreams about work, money, home, you name it. I am really looking forward to the show tonight because it is going to be *No. 1 In Heaven*, disco's highpoint in its rather short history. I am taking my wife's best friend, Rosa, to the show tonight because she wants to see this album performed live. Rosa was one of the reasons that I went to the exhibit at the Onyx coffee shop by the Vista

Theater in Silver Lake, and ended up meeting my wife.

ROSA WAS THE PERFORMER/POET and Lun*na did the costumes. They worked as a team at the time, and somehow made it to the Onyx for an exhibition of Lun*na's overly theatrical clothing and Rosa's performance, which, if memory serves me correctly was her singing with an accordion. I was struck by the spectacle of the show that night. Two Japanese women working as one artistic being. Each one had a role to play and each one was focused on the performance as well as the aesthetic. Both were incredibly beautiful. I met my future (and current) wife that night, and I wasn't looking for anything except to be amused for a couple of hours. Now many years later I am staying in Rosa's home, which she shares with her young son, Oscar. My only outing with them is breakfast or an occasional lunch at the Mozart Café near their home in North London.

ONE OF THE BEST things in my life was watching Rosa's face during the performance tonight. She was totally into it emotionally and physically. And when I looked around at the crowd, they were just as into it. The audience tonight was mostly gay men. Because *No. 1 In Heaven* is an album full of disco sound, it looked and felt like a gay disco in the seventies. In many ways it was. The audience makeup and vibe was supremely different than the previous nights. Carling Academy was changed from a haven for mainly straight loners to Studio 54.

Along with Donna Summer and Kraftwerk, Sparks is viewed as the guiding light of electronica pop music. And it all came down to this one album *No. 1 In Heaven*. Soft Cell, Pet Shop Boys, and many others like them based their sound and aesthetic on that of Sparks. Ron and Russell heard Donna Summer's "I Feel Love" and sensed a way to get out of the monotony of guitar, bass, and drummer band arrangements. Smartly, they hired Giorgio Moroder, the father of electronica and Donna Summer's producer, to produce this album.

Moroder expresses a world without borders. It's a sound for the masses, not typically what Sparks aims for, but somehow they accomplished it on this album. The beauty of *No. 1 In Heaven* lies in the tension between the interior world of Sparks and the open world of Moroder. Moroder's production doesn't interfere with Sparks' aesthetic and Moroder adds his touches to the meal without overpowering the chef's vision.

Nothing in a Sparks song goes simply from A to Z. My life in a sense has always been in the Mael brothers hands. Not as a compass, but more because I use their music to measure my standards with respect to my own work, my publishing house, TamTam Books, and generally what it means to be an artist in our culture at this very moment. Their self-containment is not only for aesthetics, but also because Ron and Russell really only trust each other artistically. Sure they let people in to produce, and to play with sound, but at the end of the day Ron and Russell have each other's backs. This gives them a sense of control and the ability to manage their career in a way that fits them as a duo.

The collaboration between Moroder and the Mael brothers must have been an encounter that they all knew would work out. At the time it was weird for Sparks fans, the band's move toward electronics and away from the electric guitar was not especially welcome. Sparks rock fans saw the synthesizer as a tool made by the devil's hands, but the electronics takes that world into the future.

The album starts out light, with a song about a sperm fighting to live, but ends up in death with "Number One Song In Heaven," a darkly comedic song that expresses their anger and disgust while being disguised in their beautiful melodies.

IF SPARKS RECORDINGS MAKE me think or feel a certain amount of pain then the live shows are pure unadulterated bliss. The audience sings the words with great abandon. When performed live the darkness of the songs seems to be kept under wraps, the joy of the live show overpowering any melancholy that otherwise seeps through the music. Perhaps this is why I have so much fun with Rosa at the show. Is there anything more wonderful than seeing a great show with a wonderful woman?

THROUGHOUT THE SHOWS, SPARKS have done little things to honor specific nights and albums. For tonight's show Ron colored his mustache and redid his hair to look like it did in 1979. From a distance I thought he was wearing a wig, but when I saw him backstage I realized it was his own hair. There is something ageless about Ron and Russell, and when I saw Ron backstage, for a brief second I thought I was back in 1979.

TERMINAL JIVE (1980)
MAY 27, 2008
ENCORE: "SINGING IN THE SHOWER"

The famous essayist Charles Lamb lived right across the street from the venue where Sparks is playing on Chapel Market. Chapel Market is an open air market with booths that have been that way ever since 1868. Lamb lived on Chapel Market with his sister Mary, who was criminally insane and convicted of killing their mother with a knife in their flat there. She wasn't sent to prison because of her insanity (both brother and sister suffered from mental illness) and because Charles agreed to take responsibility and care for her.

THE BROTHER AND SISTER never married and lived together until Charles's death. She outlived him by a decade. Both were considered to be the first Shakespearean experts or critics—he handled the tragedies and she handled the comedies. They had a full and exciting social life on Chapel Market. They held a salon with intellectuals like Samuel Taylor Coleridge, Percy Bysshe Shelley, William Hazlitt, and Leigh Hunt, where they discussed their deeply held beliefs about the pros of progressive politics in England.

Ron and Russell are in many ways similar to Charles Lamb and his sister. There are siblings who can't wait to be away from each other, and then there are those who stay together as a unit, set apart from the masses. The Lambs were in their own world of Shakespeare, madness, and their small but influential social circle. Ron and Russell seem to follow that same pattern.

If the Lambs specialized in Shakespeare then the Mael brothers are masters of the hearts and minds of the male species. Shakespeare's literature exposed the system of power within the families and high courts of Europe, where Ron and Russell specialize in outsiders. There is always a thin line between charming and creepy with respect to the characters in Sparks' songs.

Shakespeare allows an audience member to identify with all the characters onstage, as they are, in many ways, tropes of human behavior, but one is never sure how a character is going to be in a Sparks song. Their alienation is too strong and unpredictable.

TONIGHT, SPARKS PLAYED *TERMINAL Jive* from beginning to end. I used to loathe the production by Harold Faltermeyer and Moroder on the record. Faltermeyer is basically responsible for all the bad soundtracks of the eighties. *Beverly Hills Cop* is one that particularly sticks out in my mind. I think Sparks fans were worried about *No. 1 In Heaven* and the direction they were heading—I am afraid that fear had some merit. In two words: *Terminal Jive*.

THE TITLE ITSELF IS a dead give away. It's almost like Sparks wanted us to know that there is trouble ahead. Maybe it was a cry for help? When you read the lyrics of the album, it is almost shocking to compare it with any of the older Sparks songs. For example:

They make L.P. Records
And a few make comebacks
And the rest sell shoes to all the others
Rock and roll people in a disco world

WHAT IS SPARKS SAYING here? It still strikes me as shocking that pretty much all of the album's lyrics are throwaway lines, which Sparks can sometimes make charming, but here it's just dismal.

THE ONLY EXCEPTION ON the album is the song "Young Girls," which is so brilliantly perverse to my middle-aged male ears. Sparks sneaks this homage to the beauty of young girls in what seems to be an ocean of blandness. It's a straightforward song about loving young girls, which wasn't nearly as controversial in 1979 as it would be now. Lock up your daughters, because Ron and Russell are in town.

Terminal Jive appears to be a bland, uneventful album, but it has one piece of live dynamite in the middle. It's a package that will explode in your hands. Blood will flow with the sound of "Young Girls" in the background. Perhaps virginal blood?

BUT BEYOND "YOUNG GIRLS," this album has a weird knockoff quality. Maybe it was a contractual record and they just had no idea what to do? There is an instrumental version of "When I am With You" that is not only pointless, but a total head-scratcher as to why this is on an album, any album. But even with the mundanity of the album, *Terminal Jive* was a massive hit in France. Nothing makes sense in the world of Sparks.

NO SURPRISE BY NOW, *Terminal Jive* live somehow breathes life in to these otherwise insipid songs. The stupidest songs on the album come out brilliant, with bright Technicolor brush strokes that somehow turn them from shit to gold. After the concert, I rushed back to Hampstead to hear the album again. Is this the same music?

ONE CANNOT PRAISE HIGHLY enough the talents of Sparks' current live band. With only four months of rehearsal, these musicians shined in a way that is simply remarkable. The core band is Steven Nistor on drums, who is also a great onstage personality. He has sort of a goofy Dennis Wilson/Keith Moon vibe; Steve McDonald (of Redd Kross), who played bass or acoustic guitar for almost all the shows, has a sort of teen appeal onstage. He grins and bops his head with such enjoyment that it looks like he just found a lucky quarter somewhere on the stage. Jim Wilson on lead guitar, along with Marcus Blake on guitar and bass, have the sort of *don't mess with me* look every rock band needs. Very serious onstage, but with incredible backup vocals that mirror Russell's vocals. They can sing harmony (along with Steven and Steve) and look like choir boys who just got caught for smoking in the hallway. And finally, Tammy Glover, who has played off and on for Sparks for the last decade or so, is their remarkable percussionist. She just came onstage for two albums. *Balls* and *Lil' Beethoven*.

THE BEAUTY OF THIS band is their versatility and the kind of time travel they allow the audience to feel on that road that is Sparks' highway. All of the albums have a particular mood and instrumentation; they not only honor the original sound of the recordings, but also get into a mindset where they become the bands of whichever era they are performing on any particular night. It helps that they're all Sparks fans, but Jim is a Sparks connoisseur. He knows all the original arrangements and seems to be able to do all of this in his sleep.

Jim and company somehow manage to imbue meaning into this otherwise droll material and make it sound important onstage. Before the show I was very curious as to how the show for this album would do. It was popular in

France, but the consensus among most Sparks fans seemed to be that *Terminal Jive* was a bit of a throwaway. Surprisingly, they had a full audience, though not as large as *No. 1 In Heaven*. Still, the people here seem to really appreciate what they're hearing. I also am noticing faces that I haven't seen before tonight. Are there people out there who only prefer *Terminal Jive*? Ron, Russell, and Jim play this album like it's a lost masterpiece. Maybe it is, but I just can't see past the *Beverly Hills Cop* quality of it.

Listening to *Terminal Jive* after the live show, it seems like a different album. I went from hating it to now almost loving it. A friend of mine and I once got in an epic argument over Sparks. He claimed that there were no bad Sparks albums, and I distinctly remember bringing *Terminal Jive* up as a counter-argument. Now I think I may have to concede the point. If Sparks can make *Terminal Jive* a worthwhile album, there's no music I wouldn't trust in their hands.

THE ENCORE THEY DID tonight was "Singing in the Shower," which is a song they did with the great French pop band Les Rita Mitsouko. Last December (2007) the male member of this duo, Fred Chichin, passed away from cancer. I may be in love with the other half of the band, the dynamic performer Catherine Ringer. She's tough, and the closest person alive that comes close to touching the greatness of Édith Piaf. She's not Édith, but she comes pretty damn close.

WHOMP THAT SUCKER (1981)
MAY 28, 2008
ENCORE: "GO CRAZY"

It has been noted previously in this book—and elsewhere—that Ron Mael is a mixture of Adolph Hitler and Charlie Chaplin, in a visual sense. And, as I mentioned, it struck me as more than a coincidence that in 1915 Chaplin performed at a music hall theater that was around the corner from the Carling Academy. Chaplin did a nightly show at the Collins Music Hall, right across from Islington Green, which is where, during the Plague years, citizens of London buried the diseased bodies in the park. The location is now a famous meeting area for the local citizens and people watchers where you can sit on the bench and watch London life on Upper Street. Today the street itself is a mixture of gay bars, neighborhood pubs, fast food joints, and expensive dining.

Aside from a visual resemblance, I think Ron and Chaplin share a vision of the world that must be made into subversive and subjective works of art. Chaplin and the Mael brothers basically take the canvas that's out there, and either reframe it, re-edit, or eliminate the parts that are not interesting to them

Both Chaplin and the Mael brothers' world is one where a basic emotion is twisted in order to open up another world. Ron and Russell embraced the world of synthesizers, not as an alternative to the guitar pop, but as a sound that fit in their mechanical world.

I JUST MOVED TO Kentish Town where my friend Mark lives in North London, which is really not that far from where I was staying with Rosa and Oscar. For me, it's walking distance. Mark gave me his home while he was in Greece for a film festival. The thing is, he has an elaborate security system setup and I had to learn the code, and not only that but I have to set the code in a specific timeframe, which is almost an impossible task for me. Mark was very patient to show me the house and how to secure the windows and various locks.

Mark is one of my favorites. I met him on-line on an underground film website. He has a deep interest and knowledge of American avant-garde filmmakers and their films. He was the first person to show my dad's short film, *Aleph*, in London. At the time, he was writing and putting together a book of interviews with living filmmakers regarding their lives and art. He travels to various parts of the world to re-search and see films and meet filmmakers. That being said, he was very foolish to let me stay in his home alone...with the security system.

ON MY FIRST NIGHT alone there, I went to the lo-cal market to buy a bottle of red wine. This trip has been wine-free way too much. I was planning on celebrating big-time by drinking wine and writing. As I found a wine glass in the kitchen, I poured myself a big glass of red, and then I heard a noise from across the street. I didn't want to open the door or stick my head out the window in case it was something serious outside. So I walked two stories up and went into Mark's bed-room to see what was happening down below.

Mark's carpet was white as snow, and in the dark I tripped over a blanket from his bed that was on the ground. In slow motion, the wine hit the white carpet and I couldn't help but wonder if there were any charitable shelters for those who cannot be trusted as houseguests.

KENTISH TOWN IS A great area for me because I feel invisible here. It is full of family owned shops and cafés; no Starbucks or any other chain in this neighborhood. Truly a wonderful part of London, and a good writing place for me. I set up a writing area in my bedroom and pretty much stayed there from when I woke up until I left for the concert. I did go out once to eat breakfast at the local café.

It's strange but I feel awkward ordering food in London. I have a much easier time in Tokyo or Paris, and I don't even speak a second language. But British language makes me a tad insecure, especially when it comes to ordering food. It's not that I don't like British food, because I really do. I guess maybe it's more about being called out or judged because of my American accent. I will admit that my favorite British food by far is baked beans on toast. Mark even made this for me on French bread. Fantastic meal. Kind of like the British version of Top Ramen, it's cheap and easy to make, and is an excellent staple of the British diet.

ON ONE OF THE few off nights from the shows, I went with Mark to an event at LUX, an arts organization devoted to avant-garde film and video arts. LUX just opened up a temporary gallery next door to their building in East London and had Gregg Bordowitz as the guest lecturer.

He's an interesting man. He was involved with the AIDS activist group ACT UP in the late eighties and early nineties. I always admired ACT UP for the way it conveyed its message to the world. It may have been the last great graphic arts movement dealing with the social and political issues of the day.

During Bordowitz's talk he showed Vienna and discussed the statues within the cities and what they meant to the city. He hasn't figured it out yet, but he's working on it. Very much like this book you are reading now. It's not a book of answers, but a series of questions and thoughts regarding Sparks, and my thoughts during this time that I am spending with the Sparks on their fantastic voyage.

WHOMP THAT SUCKER IS an album where the mainstream and Sparks finally meet up. There was a popular and influential radio station in Los Angeles during the early eighties that really focused on new wave music. Like the success of *Kimono My House* in London in 1974, *Whomp That Sucker* made an impression on Los Angeles and the listeners of KROQ in 1981. It is an upbeat album and it's lightness accounts for its regional success. The music is catchy like getting a cold in front of an air conditioner. One could not help tapping one's feet to the beat.

Lyrically, it's leaps and bounds better than *Terminal Jive*. Early Sparks songs were dense with the intensity of the melody with the lyric, but in the eighties most popular music was more straightforward. On this album it seems as though the band was conducting an experiment in how to get a hit; there is something clinical about the recording and the songs that seemed to be cooked up in a laboratory. All that said, this is one of my favorite albums.

BECAUSE I EXPECTED THE live show to kick ass, in the same way that the live shows of lesser albums kicked ass, the show was not a knockout for me. This seems to be a trend. The albums I'm not fond of on vinyl tend to bring out nuance in the live shows that aren't accessible on the albums, while the albums that made me fall in love with Sparks seem lacking when performed live, like there's no more meaning to squeeze out.

Going to this Sparks show is like watching a beloved film series on the big screen. It hits all your expectations and you get the hits the way you want them. Sparks' twenty-one albums in twenty-one nights is exceptional practice of that rule. When you get a ticket for a specific album, you are getting the songs from the beginning of the album to the end. The only suspenseful part is the encore. What song will it be?

Almost to the minute I know the specific album's length, making sure I get on the bus back home to Kentish Town/Hampstead Heath.

What I am seeing here is sort of a Fluxus conceptual piece where the repertoire is predictable and the art lies in how we, the audiences, cope with it. Walter Benjamin writes about the nature of the artwork when it becomes part of the mechanical process of copying and how that changes the art when it is able to be dispersed to the masses. I am sure Sparks always thought of the recording as the original format of their work. The live shows are a by-product of that work. For me, personally, I get the strongest messages out of listening to Sparks alone on my record player, it is only then I am able to get totally lost in their world. When I go to a Sparks show I am all of sudden surrounded by other people, and that changes everything. It becomes a crowd of lonely people who have a passion that is not shared with the masses outside the concert hall. I don't mind being alone, but being in a crowd full of like-minded people gets on my nerves.

Sparks attracts a certain breed of fan. Obsessive, yes. Respectful to the artists, of course. Do they think about Sparks too much on a daily basis? Most definitely. And is that a bad thing? No. There is a lot to think about.

WHOMP THAT SUCKER IS a collection of songs by one outsider for another. Unlike other Sparks albums, this one tends to be more listenable to those who are not into Sparks. The music and production draws you into their world gently.

Whomp That Sucker is the most teenage of all their albums. Not sure if it was made to connect to that age bracket, or if Ron and Russell were just trying to put off adulthood. Probably a combination of both. Rock is a world where men act like boys, and I think that is quite common for both the artist and the audience. When I was a teenager I couldn't see life beyond eighteen or nineteen as the military draft was in full force. There was a part of me that thought I might not make it much farther than my late teens. So many kids my age were dying in Vietnam, it was uncertain whether or not I would join them. In many ways this stunted my desire to grow up. Why take on those responsibilities if I was just going to be shipped to Vietnam and killed anyway?

Sparks represents a mindset that has one foot in adulthood and the other leg and both arms attached to the teenage world. The tension between the two is one of the great things about Sparks. Like the character in Cornell Woolrich's great novel *Rendezvous in Black* who smashes his wristwatch to stop time, Sparks attempts an arrest of time. *Whomp That Sucker* embraces this tension of growing up and facing certain responsibilities—something that, if we had the choice, we would rather avoid.

A BOOK I PUBLISHED, *Foam of the Daze (L'écume des jours)* by Boris Vian, carries that same theme of youth getting older and not for the better. In the novel, Colin, the main character, starts off wealthy with a beautiful lifestyle, but when he falls in love, and takes responsibility not only for the relationship but also the health of his loved one, his world literally gets smaller. Even the rooms start to shrink, and the enjoyment of life is taken over by the drudgery of work and the need to preoccupy himself with the tedium of existing day-to-day. Totally the opposite of the enjoyment of being young and carefree. *Whomp That Sucker* shares the same theme with Vian's novel: youth is passed over quickly and one has to either embrace the changes or be destroyed by those changes.

I'm not sure how the teenage audience took to this record, but as someone who was in his mid-twenties when this album came out, it pretty much described my unease of being that age and where I should go from there. What I really wanted was to go back home, and home to me was being a teenager.

THE LIVE SHOW OF *Whomp That Sucker* has turned into a giant sing-along. Every song on this album is meant for a concert hall, all the choruses are catchy as Satan's promise of a good time.

ANGST IN MY PANTS (1982)
MAY 30, 2008
ENCORE: "MINNIE MOUSE"

I spent the early afternoon walking around Camden Lock, the Melrose Avenue of London. One boring hippie-dippie shop after another. When I first came here in the eighties it was fun, but now it's pretty much the same merchandise in every shop, and the marketplace got bigger.

THE ONLY GOOD THING about my walk (besides the exercise) is that I found a used copy of Richard Allen's novel *Glam*. Allen wrote a series of books dealing with youth cultures such as mods, skins, and glam kids. The books are basically pulp novels geared to their subject matter. I also found a seventies paperback copy of *The Gary Glitter Story* by George Tremlett at the used bookstore in Camden called *Black Gull Books*.

I thought Glitter's story would be interesting so I bought it. I would read this book before going to bed—it seemed to be a reasonable book to read while in London. Glitter, according to this biography, is not interesting at all. But because of his interest in underaged girls, the public liked to keep tabs on him. Gary Glitter is interesting to me because of his history as a pop singer before glam made him popular for a few years. Like Bowie and Marc Bolan, he struggled for years before he found his magic and became the Glitter King. His downfall in Vietnam doesn't interest me that much. His sexual taste is not what makes him interesting, but his showbiz history is something else.

TONIGHT, THE NIGHT OF Saturday, May 31, there is great fear in the media regarding a new law that, as of June 1, drinking will no longer be permitted in public, including in the tubes and on the buses. This sounds logical to me, but apparently is not logical to the British population. There are plans for drinking parties in various tube stations and on buses. Going to the Sparks

show tonight is not going to be the most pleasant experience, is it?

THAT SAID, SPARKS IS on fire for *Angst In My Pants*
and there was again a totally new audience there
that evening. Older fans are disappearing and
young university students are replacing them.
This is the first show where I have noticed that
the audience does not fit with the date of the
album's release. Did they come to the wrong
show by accident? No. They know all the songs.
It seems that youngsters pick up on something
about this album as their own. Some Sparks
material never ages. Never part of the world, yet
always wanting to have some part of the world.
Sparks is the perfect place for us misfits, because
the music expresses the world that we want but
can't have. Come to think of it, that's a perfect
place for youth to occupy.

THROUGHOUT THE ELEVEN SHOWS so far, faces
have come and disappeared, but there is a girl
who has been to every single one. Tonight she is
dressed like Minnie Mouse for the song "Mickey
Mouse," which is on this album. My attention
is on her because she reminds me of an old girlfriend from my more pathetic school years. The

girl I see at the show looks like she walked out of my distant memory into real life. There is something either very sweet or very dangerous about her. She has been to all of these shows and is always by herself.

I sense a lot of the people here in the audience are loners by nature. One can tell because they bring a book with them and read it in the hall before the show starts. When I see this particular girl or the book fiends here I realize that I belong to this crowd that belongs to no one. There was a tinge of an urge to talk to the Minnie Mouse girl, but the fact is I don't really have an interest in her that much or care to know her world. The fact that she's here and will likely be at the other shows as well was a warm feeling for me. Why destroy a perfect moment of bliss? I will never be disappointed and therefore always will be in an afterglow.

I HAVE A VERY strict dress code for this trip. All black. Not original, I know, but very practical. Before I left for Paris I purchased seven long-sleeved black t-shirts, one pair of black Levi's, various underpants from Muji Paris, a black hooded sweater, and a pair black and white Converse. I also cut my hair very short. I didn't want any hair problems or to even think about appearance while I was on this trip. I am here on a mission and therefore I must dress appropriately.

IT'S INTERESTING TO SEE how the audience interacts with the music onstage. Most know all the words to the songs and they are totally into the show and nothing else. They're not chitchatting (thank God) with each other, except to make a quick comment on what's happening onstage. Sparks fans are unique in that there is something private about them, like the Minnie Mouse girl who is dressed up that way not for someone else, but for herself. She is a person who is totally lost in her private world; I presume Sparks supply the soundtrack to her life. A Sparks fan just gets it. They don't need to have Sparks to explain their aesthetic.

Walt Disney is an important figure in the Sparks' world. There are at least two specific songs dealing with Disney—"Mickey Mouse" and "Minnie Mouse." Disney was a man with a plan. He single-handedly created and transformed a world within a world.

Whether one likes him or not (and I am not crazy about him) he made a place that had its own logic (Disneyland) and a world where childhood never ends. On the surface Disney is a children's figure, but grown-ups tend to have a strong emotional pull to Mickey & Co. as well.

I have only been to Disneyland once, when I was eight years old. The amusement park is exactly the same age as me, so my existence in a sense has always been tied to Disneyland. I can't imagine a world without Disneyland. I remember watching the Mickey Mouse Club on television and playing the soundtrack to Disney's version of *Zorro* on a Disney portable record player when I was a kid.

The one and only trip to Disneyland I have ever taken is permanently etched in my brain. I remember going there with my mom and my grandmother, Martha. My favorite part of Disneyland was the gift shop on Main Street where my mom and her mom bought me glass statuettes of Peter Pan and Captain Hook. The size appealed to me at the time because of Tinkerbell, who I had a crush on.

Disney's *Peter Pan* was always the most interesting to me. A child's unwillingness to grow up and take on responsibility affected me well into my twenties. In the beginning of this book, I mentioned my fear of growing up, which is, in many ways, the thing that most attracts me to Sparks. They refuse to grow up in a world not of their making. Like Peter, there is no natural home for Sparks.

SPARKS IN OUTER SPACE (1983)
MAY 31, 2008
ENCORE: "SPORTS"

While walking home from the show tonight it struck me that there is a noticeable difference between the youth of London and the youth in Paris. The youth culture in Paris has a fascination with what is both inside and outside their world. There is a sense of openness, but it's filtered through a Parisian sense of curiosity and sensibility. London, on the other hand, despite its multicultural makeup, is surrounded by a hard attitude toward city life and with that an undercurrent of violence.

Post-war Britain's theater, literature, and cinema movements, "Kitchen Sink Realism" with its Angry Young Men, still speak truthfully for contemporary London's working class citizens. In London, class distinction is noticeable, though as a foreigner it's hard for me to truly understand the difference and importance between the classes. In fact, the class structure is one that is a total head scratcher for me, but is very fundamental in British culture.

As I write this today, it is June 1, the first day beginning the new ban of open alcohol aboard public transportation. Last night was a huge party of sorts where Londoners (mostly young) invaded the tube trains to celebrate/protest the beginning of the ban. On the one hand I think, *Well why not have a drink on the train or bus, who are you hurting?* But on the other hand, alcohol does crazy things to people.

TONIGHT IN LONDON WAS another *Los Angeles* album. There are four in this series that made a huge dent on the L.A. radio stations as well as on MTV. They were also the albums that gave Sparks mainstream attention in the U.S. These are sophisticated songs clothed in a white t-shirt and blue jeans for the American audience. And the masses in America, who were fans of the new wave, ate it up.

SPARKS IN OUTER SPACE is an album I don't love. But I love the artists behind it. So it's sort of the cousin in the family that you want to slap on the side of the head to shut up, but there is a certain amount of love in that slap.

For one, it is another quintessentially eighties production. It was slightly dated even then and it doesn't go forward to another dimension like *No. 1 In Heaven*. It's electronic percussion imitating real drums. Live, the band gives the material new life. But basically the material on this album has no poison, when the best Sparks songs usually have a sense of humanity with a side dish of poison.

Sparks was trying to let the listeners catch up to them, instead of going forward. But on the other hand this was their most successful album sales-wise in the United States. Maybe they were on to something?

Culturally speaking, the band knew it was stuck in an era that was no good. You can hear it in the songs. Even though it is in its own crazy shacked-up world, Sparks still expresses what is or was happening outside the studio window. "Cool Places" was a big Sparks song that hit the mainstream at the right time. A duet with The Go-Go's Jane Wiedlin, the song has never been a favorite of mine. It's too throwaway for my taste. It totally misrepresents the Sparks' aesthetic. It's cute without the sharp wit of a toxic touch. I find it too easy. The tension is just not there.

Sparks in Outer Space is not a masterpiece, but still there are some fun songs on this album. Onstage, Sparks can make this work shine. There is a sincerity in the live performance that can win over any weaknesses in the songs themselves, but the album lacks in depth as many of the others do.

PULLING RABBITS OUT OF A HAT (1984)
JUNE 1, 2008
ENCORE: "CRIME AWARENESS WEEK"

What amazes me is how many of Sparks' albums I am not crazy about. *Pulling Rabbits Out of A Hat* is another of them. I loathe the production of it by Ian Little who made the record sound so 1984 (not in the Orwellian sense), a year that was generally not good for pop music. The mystery of pop was disappearing and becoming the wallpaper soundtrack to shopping malls across America.

The tinny sound of the record is what irks me the most. I don't like keyboards that imitate brass sounds or guitars, it reminds me how good an actual brass section sounds. The electronic drum sound is so tired-sounding after hearing it song to song. What makes it so frustrating is that there are interesting melodies on this album, which are covered up by the production. "A Song That Sings Itself" has such a beautiful melody, and in my head I hear it with a real orchestra, but instead it's lost to the murkiness of what is now called the 1984 recording.

Because of the production choices on *Pulling Rabbits Out Of A Hat*, Russell sounds constrained by the technology. Live, he releases himself, being able to proceed to the heart of the songs out of fear of falling off the tightrope. With great skill he juggles the moods in a light manner that accepts darkness as a sign of lightness and back again.

THE COMBINATION OF RUSSELL'S sweetness and Ron's darker overtones work together like dark coco in white milk. It's not a sweet taste, but it has overtures of both flavors. Russell is the vehicle for Ron's songs, similar to how Brian Wilson used to use his brothers in the Beach Boys to make music. In a sense, Ron's perfect instrument is Russell himself.

"A SONG THAT SINGS Itself" sounds like ABBA if ABBA members were raised and born in Los

Angeles. I never listened to this song properly until I heard it live. I hated this song when I first heard it, and now I have gained a genuine respect for it. If there was enough time, I think that they should re-record this album and pretend that the original version doesn't exist. But alas... And to be honest, more and better work will come out of this band, so why fret about a weak album from the past. The *Lil' Beethoven* years are just around the corner.

LYRICALLY THE EIGHTIES WERE straightforward for Sparks compared to the band's work in the seventies. *Pulling Rabbits Out Of A Hat* has more romantic themed songs, which was puzzling in respect to the prior Sparks routine of mixing lyrics with various literary allusions. Here, in songs like "With All My Might," and "Love Scenes," Sparks moved toward a more mainstream approach to romance and what it meant to the character or singer. There is none of the "Throw Her Away (And Get A New One)"—in fact, it's a different band lyrically speaking. One of the other things I dislike about the album is this change from having a very complex view of culture to one that is really trying hard to fit into that culture.

It seems like Ron was ignoring what makes him great in the first place when he wrote the lyrics to this album. Now that I have seen *Pulling Rabbits Out Of A Hat* live, I am hearing new things that I didn't pick up on first hearing the recorded album. And since seeing the live interpretation of this album, I almost love it now. Almost.

Pulling Rabbits works like throwing dry wood on top of a fire. It totally engages the audience to sing along with every pound of passion in their soul. As Noël Coward once commented, "Extraordinary how potent cheap music is." I don't see this statement as criticism of cheap music, but as praise for the mysterious way it has of conveying a feeling to listeners. When you are in the middle of Sparks' audience, you can feel Russell and Ron's magnetic hold on that crowd. No one there is thinking of their jobs or the bills that have to be paid, they are totally focused on what is happening on the stage and being there for the moment. The skill of Sparks is to specialize in obtaining and keeping those moments for the audience.

A moment is achieved when the artist has created and that creation is met with acceptance of critics or an audience—hopefully both at the same time. David Bowie's big moments are the Ziggy Stardust years and his *Low*/Berlin years. This is not to say that Bowie otherwise made terrible or unpopular music, but simply that those two or three albums define him as an icon and therefore are his masterpieces.

Every artist that has a moment must deal with that moment for the rest of their career. For Sparks, I think we all would agree, it was the Island record label years. And they have basically been trying to deal with that point of time since then. Either competing against or trying to extend that period.

SAYING THAT, *PULLING RABBITS Out Of A Hat* is not one of thier greatest albums. It is a music that is studied yet not lived. Not until one sees them do the *Rabbit* material live, can one develop a bit of an appreciation for this album. On vinyl it's dead, and though it swings live, it does not have that same transcendent feeling that the other mediocre albums had.

I HEAR COMPROMISE ON this album, and I hate the idea of artists compromising for the radio, their audience, or even with themselves. It's important for an artist to set their world apart from the others—and normally this is what made Sparks great. It's the independence and strong vision, which has made Sparks a success in many people's eyes. And though the band has never had a worldwide hit, it has made twenty-one albums, all of which are still in print. That I think is quite a remarkable feat.

MUSIC THAT YOU CAN DANCE TO (1986)
JUNE 3, 2008
ENCORE: "CHANGE"

F eeling a little bit weary with a touch of depression, I went to Soho on the West End to clear my head. London, like Los Angeles, can feel contradictory because of its diversity of neighborhoods. To me, the West End is like a movie set. Whenever I am in Soho I think of the film *Expresso Bongo* by Val Guest, based on the short story by Wolf Mankowitz, which in turn was a musical based on his story set in the West End. Andrew Loog Oldham, a huge fan of *Expresso Bongo*, hired Mankowitz's son Gered to photograph his classic band The Rolling Stones throughout the early sixties.

In the film Laurence Harvey played the hustler/manager who discovers Cliff Richards' character at a coffee bar in Soho, London. The film was made in 1959, when there was a ton of music activity in Soho. Most of it taking place at the now-legendary 2i's Coffee Bar on 59 Old Compton Street.

I STOPPED BY THE coffee bar location, which is the actual place that inspired the film and story. It is now an expensive bar and restaurant, but they have a plaque that says this is the location of the birth of British rock and roll. It is where the British rock star turned West End stage star Tommy Steele was discovered. I believe his discovery was the basis for the fictional *Expresso Bongo*. Like an idiot, I stood in front of the plaque to feel the vibe, which is not there anymore. Still, with my interest in pre-Beatles British rock and roll, it was fantastic just to stand on the pavement that Cliff, Tommy, Fury, and Vince Taylor stood on.

In the fifties various visionaries opened coffee shops specifically young people as an alternative to the age restricted bars. The birth of modern teenage culture was to kick in the big time. So coffee houses like 2i's became the CBGB's of early British rock, mostly skiffle music that was a combination of rockabilly and folk. It was basically American music filtered through a British sensibility. The low tech and no volume setup was perfect for coffee houses like the 2i's. The typical skiffle lineup would be acoustic guitar, washboard, banjo, tea chest bass, fiddle, and anything homemade that made a sound of some sort. The actual 2i's was located in the basement of a restaurant. With very little room to stand or even to breathe, these places were essential for young talent to hang out with all the great rock and roll managers—the hustlers of that time.

For me, pre-Beatles British rock holds a gritty glamorous view of London. My London is a combination of the *Carry On* films, Dirk Bogarde's early film career, Patrick Hamilton novels, the writings of Wolf Mankowitz, and Soho legend Julian Maclaren-Ross, the film *Performance* (although in the late sixties its roots are in late fifties/early sixties Soho gangster life), and Billy Fury with his generation of British rockers.

London is, in many ways, a character in a novel, especially in the works of Hamilton and Maclaren-Ross. With the mixture of American rock culture with the British mind-set, a series of explosions were set in the Soho landscape.

The gritty side of Soho is a mystical space but of course the time has changed, but still I have the movie and literature memories while walking down its streets.

The basis of contemporary British pop came from the great visionaries/hustlers of the fifties like Joe Meek, Larry Parnes, Mickie Most (sixties pop producer who also actually played at 2i's), and managers such as Andrew Loog Oldham, Simon Napier-Bell, and Kit Lambert, who eventually set the sixties on fire. In a very real sense these gentlemen placed the foundation and were the builders of a youth culture, as well as being fascinating characters themselves. They took hustling as an art form and saw their artists as not only in terms of pounds or dollars, but also perhaps as extensions of themselves. They were quirky as hell, and quite eccentric in their nature. The very basis of pop music is eccentricity. And the definition of eccentricity is Sparks.

The Mael brothers are, perhaps, the last of the great visionaries in pop. Not hustlers by nature, they do not usually compromise, and when they do, it's bad for their music and their commercial appeal. *Music That You Can Dance To* sounds like a collection of songs that don't belong together on an album.

In the eighties, Sparks had a series of bad moments. The band was going along with the times instead of reacting with its own instincts against a decade of emptiness. That's how a band makes an album like *Music That You Can Dance To*.

MUSIC THAT YOU CAN *Dance To* is not a good Sparks album by any means, but it does have a really good song (the album's title) and one masterpiece, "Change." Compared to the rest of *Music That You Change To*, "Change" is a big budget epiphany. When it is placed as part of this album it makes the rest of the songs sound like low budget B movies, something Ed Wood would have put together from various scraps that were left from other music pieces. And being true to their series of shows, they perform "Change," which was just supposed to be a single, as their encore for this particular tribute to this album.

I find myself wondering if there is such a thing as a fan that only loves *Music That You Can Dance To*? Strange in a beautiful way, the answer is yes. I'm guessing that this audience may not be familiar with *Kimono My House* and waited for this show with a dying breath—because, now at last, the full version of *Music That You Can Dance To* is on live onstage. Fans of eighties music are a weird bunch to me. They're young tonight, mostly in their twenties and early thirties. Perhaps *Music That You Can Dance To* is the classic album from that era to these kids. What a strange audience?

SPARKS CAN TURN SHIT into gold when they play music on the stage. As I mentioned, my favorite shows have been the albums that I don't like that much. I've never seen a series of concerts like this one, but also, I'm being re-exposed to works that I didn't care about and haven't listened to in a long while, so perhaps it's unsurprising that I have been finding hidden gems in the music. Mind you the songs are not terrible, just not up to the Sparks standard.

One of the reasons this album sounds so disjointed is that some of the songs were meant for other projects that didn't happen. Two of the songs, "Modesty Plays" (a play on *Modesty Blaise*, but Sparks couldn't use the name due to copyright law) and "Armies of the Night," were written for films that were never produced. There is a useless cover of Stevie Wonder's "Fingerprints" that gives an

unclear picture of where the album was headed and the purpose of it.

I GOT MY FIRST real job in the eighties. I started to
work at a record store. Licorice Pizza was a chain
store that was a big part of the Southern California landscape. It was the height of the record
business, and I witnessed the big change from
vinyl, to cassettes, to CDs. I served two locations
with Licorice Pizza. One was in Reseda, a few
miles away from the capital of pornography, and
the other was in West Los Angeles, on Wilshire
Boulevard. That was a very pleasant place to
work with a fantastic staff.

I have very fond memories of Steve, Jim,
and Paul (the employees of the store), because
we shared a culture that was important to us,
one of the few times in my life where I felt I
could share my love with people who understood, they got the importance of the records
and the shows. We may not have agreed on particular recording artists, but we understood the
passion behind it.

So when I look at the cover for *Music That
You Can Dance To*, I think of these lads and
ladies. And the album entices me to think
of the pleasures that lurk within me, and the

romances that were started by our common interest in music and books. *Music That You Can Dance To* didn't open doors for me, but it was clearly in the background of pleasures and that's all I can ask for.

INTERIOR DESIGN (1988)
JUNE 4, 2008
ENCORE: "BIG BRASS RING" & "LIKE THE MOVIES"

To clear my head before the show tonight I went back to Soho to walk around in the warm weather. Soho is a powerful magnet, and I always come back to the same spot and usually around the same time of the late afternoon. The best time to go is around 4:00 P.M. so I can see the change from daylight to nighttime. The neighborhood at night. People start pouring into all the bars around 6:00 P.M. Soho is the entertainment area of London. God knows how much liquor is drunk in this rather small, but complex area. Here it's usually the after-work crowd. White collar with a mixture of secretaries and well-to-do gentlemen added as eye candy and a sense of relief after a workday. At the very least there are twenty-six gay bars in Soho, which is approximately one square mile in length.

I try to wrap my brain around these streets that have an emotional pull for me. It is easy for me to time travel to the fifties and imagine running into Gerald Kersh (the author of *Night and the City*) and perhaps the great photographer John Deakin, a friend of Francis Bacon, lurking in the shadows selling dirty photographs of one of Bacon's models. But no, instead I run on the streets of Soho with office workers which makes me feel a bit blue.

I POPPED INTO A bookstore and found various books about Soho as well as an interesting little biography on *Carry On* comedian and actor Charles Hawtrey. A tragic yet fascinating character. Reading the biography by Roger Lewis, one would think it will be an amusing narrative, but it turns very dark and extremely sad by the end of his life. A chronic alcoholic, trapped in a society that legally did not accept homosexuals, Hawtrey expressed himself as a prissy character in the *Carry On* films, which perhaps masked his disgust with the world around him.

MOST OF LONDON MAKES me feel lonely. There are so many couples going out and having fun. And yours truly has only a Moleskine notebook for a companion. But this is not a complaint. Solitude in a big city is something I actually crave. There is something beautiful about being lost in a crowd—especially in the streets of a major city like London.

WHEN I AM AT the Sparks shows, there is another gentleman who is at the show by himself like me. He too has been to every show. I like him from a distance because he is usually reading a book before the show, either in the lobby, where they are selling the merchandise and the lighting is good for reading, or inside the venue itself. I never approach him because it looks like going to a Sparks show is a very private activity for him. I feel that way, too. And being lonely at a show is very much like wearing a nice coat to keep you warm and away from trouble. I am also not that crazy about sharing my experiences at a show or listening to a record unless I am writing about it. Odd? Yes, but the intensity of getting the music directly is something mysterious and powerful. If I had my choice, it would always be going to a show alone. Sparks is the perfect band or artist for the solitary individual.

INTERACTING WITH SPARKS IS not the same as interacting with someone like Bruce Springsteen or the Grateful Dead, which is more about the community that the band creates. Sparks is not about community; it's about being away from any community.

To be alone is not the worst thing that can happen to a chap. I believe solitude is a Zen way of living among all the clutter and confusion that is out there. What Sparks wants is to be left alone. And that is the irony, that pop music is a medium to attract a community of sorts but the Mael brothers just want to be left alone to do art. They want the audience, but they don't really make music for the masses.

IT's ODD TO SEE Sparks fans interact with each other. A lot of them have met previously during the series of shows. The usual fan websites post discussions on subjects such as *The best Sparks songs in order of greatness* or *The worst Sparks' songs in order of horribleness*, so a lot of us hardcore fans know each other from those debates, which are endless and don't tell you what the band is about or why one should care or not care about this or that song; it just highlights the obsessiveness of Sparks fans.

I IMAGINE *INTERIOR DESIGN* is listed in the *Huh?* category of Sparks albums. Like *Music That You Can Dance To*, *Interior Design* doesn't really form a cohesive unit, but is an album trying to hook up with the times.

The *Interior Design* show was good, not great, though I fell in love with two songs on the album that I previously disliked. "A Walk Down Memory Lane" has a haunting melody, but when I hear it now, it brings me back to the loneliness of walking in a darkened Soho. The beautiful, unapproachable girls. The young urbanites drinking at fancy bars. The theatergoers scuttling to their musicals. When I heard this song, it was like I was out of Islington, out of Los Angeles, and right into the crowded narrow streets of Soho.

The opening lines:

> *We all expected champagne*
> *But it never did come*
> *But it never did come*
> *We said, "Hey, where's our champagne?"*
> *And they gave us a gun*
> *Said to go and have fun*
> *So many riches just out of reach*
> *Coming attractions washed up on the beach, oh yeah*

MORE ABOUT MEMORY EITHER being placed or forced upon its characters, Sparks leaves out the phenomenon of nostalgia, as if a walk down memory lane takes place on a completely different plane than that misappropriation of memory.

> *Let's take a walk*
> *A walk down memory lane*
> *Past the signs of the times*
> *That lit our little way*
> *And decide what it is*
> *That made it all this way*
> *And decide who it is*
> *That might make it O.K.*

"Madonna" is the other song on *Interior Design* that this show managed to awaken. It's about a guy who is picked up by Madonna while walking down the street. Based on a sort of urban myth that was going around in the eighties, it was reported that Madonna used to pull up to gentlemen on the street and pull them into her limo for sex. It sounds wonderful, but I'm sure it's not.

Recently, when I was studying up on my Sparks albums in preparation for these twenty-one nights, I was seduced by another song off this album "You've Got A Hold Of My Heart," which did nothing for me for years, and now draws me to it for some reason. Sparks songs are kind of like those books that you have to read at just the right point in your life. There are songs that are like *Catcher In The Rye* that you can only appreciate in your youth, and then there are songs that you have to have a certain amount of life experience to understand. "You've Got A Hold Of My Heart" needs some life experience behind it in order to connect. It is a scorned lover narrative, but the melody acts in direct opposition to the words—it is a jaunty number that doesn't properly convey the disappointment in the lyrics.

Again, a bright and hopeful melody goes against the disappointment of the lyrics.

THE REST OF THE songs on the album are only okay. The live show breathes some life into them, but there's only so much Sparks can do.

GRATUITOUS SAX & SENSELESS VIOLINS (1994)
JUNE 6, 2008
ENCORE: "MARRY ME"

Goodbye troubled eighties and let the good times roll into the nineties. *Gratuitous Sax & Senseless Violins* brings back the idea of a classic Sparks album. It was the first step of their great resurgence in pop music. What they lost in the mid-eighties came back around in the nineties. It seems Sparks retreated back into their world instead of trying to fit into some other world of pop music, a world they often seemed to be aiming for in the eighties albums.

GRATUITOUS SAX & SENSELESS *Violins* is a totally underrated album, and the live show makes my argument as to why this album is so important. Sparks' wit and sense of adventure all comes together on this album, redefining their culture instead of allowing outside forces to heap on compromise.

Two songs at the performance tonight frame the album and the show: "Gratuitous Sax" and "Senseless Violins." "Gratuitous Sax" is just a multitracked vocal song, in the vein of "Propaganda," that jumps into Euro-pop. The beauty of this record is that it goes against everything that was happening musically in 1994. Anathema to Grunge, *Gratuitous Sax & Senseless Violins* predicted the Ace of Base style pop music that hit the scene in the nineties. "Gratuitous Sax" is not saying *fuck grunge*, more like saying; *this is not my world, but this is the world as I know it.* And it's that independence that was missing in the last couple of Sparks' albums.

"THE GHOST OF LIBERACE" is both a tribute to the man as well as a joke about the more ridiculous aspects of him. There is genuine sympathy for Liberace, perhaps Ron and Russell see him as a man like themselves, outside the mainstream, flamboyant in ways not always understood by the majority of people.

"The Ghost of Liberace" really touches me and I am not exactly sure why. I suspect that there is a Liberace lurking in my soul. He was a man who had to sort of hide himself in plain sight; I often feel that, as the public face of my father's estate, as the publisher of Boris Vian, I store myself in plain sight. Like Sparks, I live in my own world, only inhabiting what I must of the real world in order to maintain and survive.

Whenever I go to Las Vegas, I go and visit the Liberace Museum (since closed, sadly), which is in a great little place in a depressing strip mall. But like most great things, one can find beauty in the strangest places. I found a lot of beauty in the Liberace Museum. Most of the costumes are handmade and the detail of the clothing is first rate. There are no short cuts with respect to the best material and jewelry in the makeup of the costumes. When you see it laid out in an exhibition, it's incredibly impressive. His jewelry collection can be seen as excess, but I see him as an individual who wanted to change his world from something bleak into something beautiful. Liberace physically changed the world around him to serve his purpose, aesthetic, and desire. He's basically an eighteenth/nineteenth century dandy.

PERHAPS WITH THEIR TWENTY-ONE nights Sparks are primed to achieve, if not the same notoriety as Liberace, the same goals as Liberace. Parlaying their discography into a more tangible expression of beauty. Or perhaps this is just a comment on fandom. I mean, how many other bands would embark on something this massive, and how many other fans would come to watch twenty-one full albums? Every single song, not just the singles and fan favorites. When I go to describe it, it sounds nuts. But then, maybe that's what it takes to be a Sparks fan.

There is something obsessive and slightly off base in going back and redoing your own work. This series of shows in London are being redone but not heavily rearranged. The songs stay as close as possible to the original recordings. What really impresses me is all instruments onstage are live. The *Plagiarism* and *Indiscreet* shows featured a live string section onstage with them. Sparks didn't cut any corners in re-doing its catalog onstage. The concerts work as a conceptual art piece as well as a concert series.

GRATUITOUS SAX & SENSELESS *Violins* was Sparks' first album after taking a break from public life for five years. During the missing years they had been trying to put together a film based on a Japanese Manga by Kazuya Kudo, called *Mai, The Psychic Girl*, which is about a young lady who has psychic powers and is being pursued by the ultra-evil Wisdom Alliance. Mai was one of the first mangas to be translated into English and still has a following in the English-speaking world. Ron and Russell wrote a whole film score for this film that still hasn't been made, unfortunately.

UP TO THIS POINT and compared to the other albums, *Gratuitous Sax & Senseless Violins* is Sparks most adult record. Here I feel the Mael brothers are middle-aged and are looking through the eyes of not a youngster, but a person who has seen things and taken notice of the changes around them. This is a big turning point for Ron and Russell's writing. As their work progresses after this album, it is clear that Sparks started seeing things in a new light. Gone are the days of mundane and monotonous lyrics. Instead, Sparks starts speaking toward the trajectory of humanity and human emotion.

PLAGIARISM (1997)
JUNE 7, 2008
ENCORE: "LOOKS AREN'T EVERYTHING"

had the strangest dream last night. I was in a house somewhere on the Sunset Strip (that alone is strange) and the house started to cry. Every room in this large house was crying. It sounded like a middle-aged woman, which, for some reason, reminded me of someone I used to know. Her tears would wake me up in the middle of the night, and I'd just pretend that I didn't hear her. The crying was from the gut, and this dream conveyed the same feeling I had that night with her. I woke up feeling depressed.

I WENT TO SOHO again to clear my head and exchange my last few dollars for pounds. While walking around this neighborhood I found a great record store, and not even looking at the sign outside, I walked in. Thereafter, I realized I was in Sounds of the Universe, which houses Soul Jazz Records. This label always impressed me because they re-released many classic dub reggae recordings, as well as various post-punk and New York no wave underground bands such as DNA, The Contortions, and so forth.

PLAGIARISM FEELS LIKE HOME. The original concept for *Plagiarism* was as sort of a tribute album with guest artists doing their favorite Sparks songs with Ron and Russell producing the procedure. But instead, after a couple of tracks, Sparks takes over to redo several of its own songs. Rather then have *Plagiarism* be a greatest hits package, Sparks has employed its own selective memory to reclaim and reinvent their past, and somehow make it all new. Sort of the theme of the whole twenty-one nights.

Sparks began rehearsals in January 2008, working everyday with only Sunday's off. 9:00 A.M. to 5:00 P.M., Monday through Saturday with an hour lunch break and snacks in between. I gather this is their regular work schedule, even when they're not preparing for twenty-one shows. They go on holidays, but it's like a vacation from their regular job of being Sparks.

They are now on their seventeenth album with these series of shows, and still have to rehearse daily. Plus future shows will have some theatrics associated with them, meaning there will be tech dress rehearsals as well. The hard work doesn't stop.

THESE SHOWS IN LONDON are a highly conceptual work of art, not for only the artists onstage, but for the audience as well. For the hardcore fan to see every performance takes a certain amount of money, time, and persistence. As a member of the audience we are not seeing any surprises here on the stage. The only surprise that is allowed for this series of shows is the encore. It is hard to guess what the song will be because it is normally a B side to a single that was recorded about the time of that particular album, or an unused track made for a film or television. What we do know is the opening song and the song order of that night's set. The arrangements will be the same or very close to the recordings, so no surprise there. These are a series of shows for an audience who hates surprises.

THE DRAMA FOR THE audience is the endurance of doing such a show, it is like a job where you clock in for the performance and then clock out afterward. Not literally, mind you, but in theory and practice only. You get there at 7:00 P.M., hand over your ticket (like punching a time clock), then leave at the same time. And then you do the same the next day. It's a highly unusual format with respect to going to a show. Rock and roll as a factory.

Sparks does the same. The band shows up, rehearses, eats, then performs. It does this every day for these series of shows, and so does the audience members who go to all the shows. I usually eat at the local Wagamama, and consistently see members of the audience as well as the band eating at the same location and at the same time. It's an odd world where one treats an event or art show as a work schedule.

I have a routine for these shows and writing sessions. I get up around 8:30 A.M., take a shower, a shave every three days (to save money on shaving equipment), and then make myself some instant coffee. I write for two or three hours, break away and read various books, such as *King's Road* by Max Décharné and Spike Milligan's WWII memoir, *Monty: His Part in My Victory*. I also bought a collection of memoir essays by Julian Maclaren-Ross and a small biography by Roger Lewis on the British character actor and comedian Charles Hawtrey.

It's important for me to surround myself with British books and music while I am here writing about Sparks because I need to isolate myself as much as possible to get into a mind-set where I am surrounded by the subject of Sparks and interests around that subject matter. I like to think of it as method writing.

PLAGIARISM IS BOTH A copy and remake of their past. There is a natural tension between the past and the present. And because of Sparks' career longevity, there will be always differences in opinion of what the audience expects of them.

By the very first song on *Plagiarism*, it becomes clear that this is the sound of twenty-first century Sparks. Orchestrated pop, art-like chamber pieces, with big orchestrations. The first song, "Pulling Rabbits Out Of A Hat" was a terrible song on the first album. But here it becomes something grand and almost desperate.

The rest of the songs on *Plagiarism* are not all that different from the original recordings of the songs. My guess is that Sparks wasn't trying to curb disapproval of the original recordings, but to revisit many of the songs with new eyes. Most of the arrangements bring out a superficial dandyish flourish

There is something absurd about recording an album like this, but the live show is borderline insane. *Plagiarism* is an updated résumé to show listeners/consumers what Sparks is all about. In one hour a complete picture of Sparks is created.

With the help of Tony Visconti, Erasure, Faith No More, and Jimmy Sommerville, *Plagiarism* is a unique and wonderful album from Sparks. But for those who followed them from the very beginning it still comes out like a new work. The songs are old but the music is new, a mixture of awe and nostalgia.

BALLS (2000)
JUNE 8, 2008
ENCORE "WHAT WOULD KATHARINE HEPBURN SAY?"

B *alls* is not a great album. Not necessarily due to the quality of the individual songs, which I think is fine, but because it does not pull together as a package. It seems to be a collection of songs looking for a home. Not sure if anyone wants to claim *Balls* as a home. One of the most beautiful songs on this album is "Scheherazade." Lyrically unusual for a Sparks song, "Scheheraza-de" follows the subject of the *One Thousand and One Nights*. A king has a penchant for killing his wives after they are no longer virgins, and one of his wives, Scheherazade, is an excellent story-teller. She tells the king stories that end in cliffhangers in order to stay alive. The king can't kill her because he would never find out the ending to her stories. It's her ability to tell stories that keeps her alive. She is literally a performer who needs to perform to have a chance.

In "Scheherazade" the lyric that really cores down to the center of the song is "There's a sameness to the world in its plainness." It so aptly captures the melancholy that is always lying just under the surface in Sparks' best songs. The precision of the lyrics and music make each song seem quite simple on one level, but they are not bright and bubbly songs, they grapple with deeper life issues, not always conveyed by the somewhat lighter music. I never find a Sparks song comforting.

I have seen Sparks as a trio singer, keyboard/computer, and drummer perform some of the songs from *Balls* before, but the addition of electric guitar and bass is an extra pleasure and much needed to flush out the songs' melodies. For Sparks just to rely on Ron's electronics and live drums makes the songs come out empty and uninteresting, but with a full band the material takes on a whole new depth.

AT THIS POINT, I am feeling a touch of sadness because the shows are coming to a close. Without a doubt, going to these series of shows is one of the greatest things I have done in my life. To investigate and think and just be in the audience is pretty amazing. Sparks is one of the few groups in the world that really push that envelope on music and what it can do and convey.

I'm starting to get concerned that I haven't done enough to make contact with the audience. I could go up to anyone start chit-chatting, but that is so not me. My life is isolated, which is the way I like it; I could easily live in Superman's Fortress of Solitude. London is similar to Superman's fabled lair, at least in my mental state. I find that the more bookstores there are the happier I am. And London still has a ton of new and used bookstores. Charing Cross Road is like my version of Mecca. I find myself meandering through musky shelves and finding little treasures, more than happy to disappear in the overcrowded aisles, hoping that the perfect book will fall on my head.

FOR AN ENCORE, SPARKS did a song I have never heard before. Shocking, I know. It seems like Ron wrote it for a singer by the name of Christie Hayden and it's called "What Would Katharine Hepburn Say?" For a song that never has been released and maybe not even recorded, it is one of their best, a beautiful ballad that sounds both lost and wishful. Four months after hearing this song it stays with me like a love letter never sent. And like that lost love letter, I kind of want to send it to Christie Hayden, whoever she may be.

LIL' BEETHOVEN (2002)
JUNE 10, 2008
ENCORE: "WUNDERBAR"

Sparks has decided to take no prisoners. In a sense, it is a now or never in regards to the legacy this series of shows will leave. *Balls* strikes me as an album that played by the rules, and the rules failed to serve Ron and Russell's ambition. On *Lil' Beethoven* they broadened their scope and started painting on a much larger canvas. The album is almost theatrical in its execution. In fact, they usually try to incorporate more theatricality into their performance when playing songs from *Lil' Beethoven*. Ron and Russell came up with a character named Lil' Beethoven who wrote these songs, which freed Sparks, and opened up a new avenue for the work.

Although the theatricality of thinking and execution on *Lil' Beethoven* might seem like a radical gesture from Ron and Russell, those traces have actually been set in place since the band started. Sparks uses their on and off Broadway musical influences to broaden and deepen their work to make lasting images on the stage and in the listener's imagination.

It is almost as if there is a movie being made, but without script, camera, or lights; your job as a listener is to close your eyes to listen to the music using your eyelids as a screen. And there waiting will be fantastic scenes directed by the Mael brothers.

The shows may be an interpretation of the songs, but they do not replace the images that are flicker through the audience's head. The album combines the Steve Reich rhythm with Chopin's classical flair. It has some bearing of Laurie Anderson as well, but it's totally filtered through the sensibility of Sparks. So although you can think, *oh I hear so-so here*, the combination of the influences, and the variety of influences, are such that only Sparks could have put them all together in order to produce that sound. It's a

Sparks world and you are welcome to stay; if you go, just gently shut the door behind you, please.

I HAVE PLAYED THIS album to friends and some of them just don't get it. The album does not have the obvious payoff one gets from regular pop music. It's music that plays with the notion of what a pop song is, and Sparks is first and foremost a pop band. Still *Lil' Beethoven* is a series of more artistic songs, the melodies are complex, and rhythms strange. But these art songs come filtered through the medium pop. It's an important distinction to make, because Sparks is very much part of the pop world by design. To this day they think of the single as an aesthetic form and a natural medium in the nature of pop. The song is everything and the album is the book.

Lil' Beethoven, the character on the album, is a streetwise youth whose great, great, great, great, great grandfather is Ludwig van Beethoven. Lil' Beethoven inherits his distant relative's genius for music and meanders through the songs like he's walking down a crowded London street.

This is the first time on any of their records that Ron Mael has written as a character. *Lil' Beethoven* is a concept album, not only because of the inclusion of a character, but also because many of the songs feature commentary on the music business. Be it the amount a musician has to practice, the constant drudgery of the business side of music, or the thrill of making it to Carnegie Hall, *Lil' Beethoven*, in many ways is an accounting of music through the eyes of Lil' Beethoven.

"My Baby's Taking Me Home" is a song that, if the stars are aligned correctly, makes me cry. It may have the most beautiful chorus in pop ever. A minimalist work of genius that is so simple the emotion of the piece lends itself to maximum intensity. Russell sings the line "My baby's taking me home" over and over again in multiple voices until it builds up into an emotional sense of bliss. I would say it's spiritual but maybe it's more faithful, the idea that there is someone out there that loves you and will embrace you. The desire to be embraced in the warmth of arms and be led into comfort.

Throughout my history with Sparks, I often think of the works by Bertolt Brecht and Kurt Weill. *Lotte Lenya Sings Kurt Weill* is my first memory of a record being played on a turntable. My parents had this album and played it on a daily basis; my German grandmother, who I often stayed with, also had this album and used to play it all the time. Lenya was married to Kurt Weill and was the original actress in *The Threepenny Opera,* and I guess my first music crush, as well. Lenya's vocals were rough and whiskey-soaked, the bittersweet melodies even more profound; in a world that was a horror show, there were traces of beauty in the scorched earth. The beautiful melody drags the listener to a comfortable spot and then the lyrics club them nearly to death.

The ugly desires the beauty. It is as old as the fairy tale, and the beauty of Weill/Brecht's songs are the mashup of ugly worlds within beautiful melodies. Sparks works in this format, as well. The band often sings about ugly events, but is always backed by a beautiful melody.

LIL' BEETHOVEN IS AN album that feels like Sparks filtered through the ghosts of Kurt Weill and Bertolt Brecht. The live version of *Lil' Beethoven* seems to be a staging of agitprop theater in its low budget production and smallish stage, which conveys a message to the masses. One imagines Orson Welles directing the stage production of this album in New York City during the late thirties. Like classic agitprop, it is a work that is meant to hit you in the head, and somehow touch an emotional base at the same time.

HELLO YOUNG LOVERS (2006)
JUNE 11, 2008
ENCORE: "PROFILE"

Tonight is the last show in Islington. I've been sad all day knowing that this is all coming to an end soon. As I walk around and talk to everyone, it seems like they're all sad it's over, too—relieved it went well, but sad that it's coming to an end. The band was rehearsing everyday for five or six hours with maybe an occasional Sunday off. It has been consistent work for them from their first day in London until now. My understanding is that they have to rehearse the new album *Exotic Creatures from the Deep*, as well as the theater set pieces that are involved in the show. The second half of the show will only be requests that were made by the fans who voted for their favorite songs on Sparks' website. Everyone is expecting obscure songs, as well as some hits. It promises to be an amazing night, musically and emotionally.

Fans sponsored certain shows in the series in Islington. Instead of going to corporations for funding for these shows, individuals or families could sponsor a particular night or album by Sparks. There was an online bidding area for that pleasure, which included getting to meet the brothers, plus a signed document of some sort.

I am quite moved by how things came together, and tonight at the *Hello Young Lovers* show I find myself tearing up in the audience. It's great when people work together for a common cause—I guess that's why people love sports so much. I'm not really a sports fan, but nevertheless I understand the high that happens when a team achieves a common goal.

I SPENT THE DAY walking around Mayfair to locate an old flat that I stayed in with my family in the summer of love, 1967. Art dealer Robert Fraser owned the flat. He was the first European to actually give notice to the art scene in

Los Angeles during the sixties. He was a charismatic figure who brought the pop music and art world together; he slummed with the lowest and had dinner with the best of society. He was an incredibly unique figure in London and Los Angeles pop culture.

Robert was one of the first people in the sixties art world to give notice to my father's work. He bought his artwork directly from my father, and ended up becoming good friends. In 1967, Fraser had a show at his gallery called *Los Angeles Now*, and my family came for the show. I don't remember the opening, but I do remember visiting his gallery; it had a spiral staircase to the basement, and I had never seen anything like it before.

Before we came to London, Robert Fraser got busted with Mick Jagger and Keith Richards for drugs. I think he was carrying heroin in his coat pocket. The Stones did very little jail time, but because Robert came from a better social class, he was made an example and had to serve six months in prison. While his life was on hold, we got his flat. Even while in prison, when he could only talk to someone once a week, he arranged for us to stay there at his flat at 23 Mount Street in Mayfair.

That address is drilled into my brain because my parents took taxis everywhere when we were in London I remember them always telling the driver, "Take us to twenty-three Mount Street please." It was an address that many cab drivers and participants of the swinging sixties knew by heart as well.

I remember we went to see Allen Ginsberg read and my dad hailed a taxi on the street. He noticed an older gentleman trying to get the same taxi as well. My dad called out to him to come and share the car with us, because at that time it was late and it was hard to get around London at nighttime past a certain hour. He got in the car, and this gentleman really looked like a gentleman, like a high-minded banker. When my dad told the driver "twenty-three Mount Street please" the extra guess said "ah, Fraser's flat." He introduced himself as William Burroughs and told my dad he had been there many times. Everyone knew everyone in those days. If you were an artist, you knew this musician, who knew this art dealer, and so forth.

As a child, Robert's flat seemed huge. What I remember the most is the bed, which had a canopy covering it. It was very decadent and dandyish, and as a child, it made quite an impression on me. Also, he had an incredible record collection, and every record was in the wrong sleeve. It was there that I first discovered the music of the Jimi Hendrix Experience, The Who's *A Quick One*, Manfred Mann, and a couple of Stax soul records. But to find a particular record, you had to check every record sleeve for that album. It was a headache for a twelve-year-old.

The fireplace had a John Lennon drawing on it. It seemed he took acid there, and started to draw on the wall. Being a Beatles fan, I was very excited to be staying in a room that contained this giant of a man, and his doodling on the wall.

WITH THOUGHTS OF 23 Mount Street flowing into my brain cells, I took a walk there from Oxford Circus. Once I found the building, I was kind of surprised that it didn't ring any memory bells for me. It is now next door to a Marc Jacobs clothing shop—all the stores on the block are upscale boutiques and restaurants now. I remembered it as a residential block with a small market that sold weird British food and even stranger comic books. I specifically remember milk cartons that didn't open like the American ones, so I kept spilling milk on my lap.

There is no trace of my past life in this part of London. For some reason I thought the flat was on the third floor, which is a private residence, but I was wrong. There aren't three floors in this building. Now they're residences. It's always sad when you realize how quickly distinct memories can change. One of the great tragedies of life is the way humanity paves over its past in an effort to move forward. I find myself trudging away from 23 Mount Street with a weight on my chest.

After my sad morning, I went to King's Road in Chelsea. This roadway is famous for the sixties swinging London, as well as Malcolm McLaren and Vivienne Westwood's shop SEX, where the Sex Pistols were first formed. I went by their shop at World's End and the iconic clock was still there, but everything else seemed to be gone. My brief adventure as a child in London is now dead; I find myself wishing that some of my childhood memories were still around. I guess that is why there are so many plaques on buildings, to remind one that something special took place there and someone special shared the air.

AFTER THE SPARKS' SHOWS, if nothing else, there should be a blue plaque outside the Carling

Academy saying "*Sparks played here and played every song in their catalog between May 16, 2008 and June 11, 2008.*" But, then again, they don't have a plaque for Keith Richards and Anita Pallenberg's house in Chelsea either. Hopefully one day they will for both.

AFTER THE SHOW I went home and had a strange dream. One would call it a nightmare, but it was also beautiful. I was with Ron, Russell, and another friend at my old house in Topanga. The mountain range in front of my house was lighted with some sort of energy or fuel burning. And in slow motion we saw rockets being blasted from the mountain range and hitting objects near my house. Russell noted that we were being attacked, but it was beautiful. All of us were calm inside the house, but we could actually see the missile flying over the house in slow motion. There would be a horrible explosion after the missiles hit their target, and it would cause the house to shake. Then we looked outside the house and saw someone shooting someone. The police came and held the victim of the shots. He was screaming in pain, and the shooter came up again and shot him again. I told Ron and Russell that I actually saw someone get shot. We were all in shock.

I woke up from this dream breathing heavily like someone was physically chasing me. The oddness of the dream stayed with me for the rest of the day.

HELLO YOUNG LOVERS IS an album that borders on the insane. It resembles *Lil' Beethoven* in form, but that is about it. If *Lil' Beethoven* is an European theater piece, then *Hello Young Lovers* comes back around to the big Broadway musical.

"Dick Around" was their single choice, which was problematic. You can't use the word "dick" on the BBC, which is the main outlet of music in the U.K., so there was some trouble even getting the song out there. "Dick Around" is about a character that lost his girl, is bitter about it, and now all he does now is dick around. With a punishing beat in parts, there is no way this song would play in the era of *The Voice*.

But beyond that, this is an album of pleading and loss. The humor is there, but it's tinged with tragedy and a giant side dish of sad melody. It's Broadway filtered through a Sparks' nightmare of a relationship. *Hello Young Lovers* brings to mind the romantic picture of Frank Sinatra hanging out in the middle of the night by a lamppost, as young lovers walk by. It is almost a deep meditation of being in the basement of despair. Sparks plays with that imagery and emotional ties to a failed relationship, but as a stage piece the emotions just get bigger. Sinatra is playing for the one loser out there, but Sparks is putting that emotion on a big-budget stage. At least that's the sound of *Hello Young Lovers*.

IT'S FUNNY BUT A few days ago I was on a bus from North London to go to somewhere in the West End, as it was a rare day off for Sparks. Looking outside my bus window I saw Marcus, Jim, and Steve, all members of the Sparks touring band, walking together on Upper Street toward Essex Road, and I couldn't help but think about what an experience like this is like for everyone. The band and the fans alike. Those band members strolling down the street, they really struck me as a band or unit walking on the street, kind of family-like, like John, George, Paul and Ringo living in the house, with separate entrances in the film *Help*.

Maybe it was because I was on a bus and I saw them from a distance, but it was a weird and great few seconds.

EXOTIC CREATURES OF THE DEEP (2008)
JUNE 13, 2008
ENCORE: "FOURTEEN SONG SET"

The last show. The last night for Sparks. I feel as though I'm headed to a wake. I actually cried in the audience—thank God for darkened theaters. Like the last two albums, the live show for *Exotic Creatures of the Deep* is very theatrical onstage and in its music. Sparks is moving into new territory and the last three albums, although very different from each other, also represent a new interest in Sparks' sound and dynamic.

The music fits perfectly with tonight's venue, Shepherd's Bush Empire, a theater built in 1903. The first performer to use the theater was

Fred Karno, who invented the pie in the face and was quoted as saying "When in doubt, fall on your arse."

Sparks explore the world of pop filtered through a vaudevillian's eyes. The essence of the pratfall usually involves something hiding much deeper in the psyche. I always felt vaudeville slapstick and war had a common relationship. Slapstick is always at war, whether it's with another person or an object of some sort.

EXOTIC CREATURES OF THE *Deep* is very different from the other albums. I think it's maybe a masterpiece. I'll have to see what their next album is like in order to properly categorize its placement in the realm of masterpiece. It's hard to separate Sparks' albums from each other. One adventure leads to another.

Clearly the same people who made *Exotic* made *Kimono My House* but the *Kimono* is made by young men, and while *Exotic* is made with life experience, and more definition as to what life entails. Sparks have grown, and in a way, I have too. Not just from that lost, angry young man who listened to *Kimono My House* with such ferocity, but also just in this past month that I've spent with Sparks. The amount of workmanship and craft that has gone into these twenty-one nights has left me breathless, awe-inspired. I'm ready to move forward in my life, and more prepared than ever to be back to my life, to inhabit it in a way that I haven't been able to or willing to before.

RUSSELL HAS A STUDIO where they can make music around the clock without worrying about the budget. For the last three or four albums, each project has taken a year to make. Ron and Russell have a factory-minded work ethic when it comes to Sparks. They meet up everyday in the morning, work through the day, and stop at dinnertime. Even their rehearsals with the band for this tour were factory-like. One can imagine the musician clocking in for the rehearsal and clocking out to go home.

AT THE END OF their live set for *Exotic Creatures*, Ron burns all the images of the album covers on the big screen onstage with a cigarette lighter.

Knowing that they spent the last forty years putting together all their albums, their life's work, and then burning them is beautiful and very Zen; one has to be free from the past while accepting that the past has taken place, and has effected the present. This series of shows serves as a narrative, and also shows a fascination with how the process started and how it ends. What I saw onstage is the ability of Sparks to call the shots within the context of its history.

Even now watching the symbolic burning on YouTube brings tears to my eyes. It reminds me of going to a cemetery for a cremation. Sparks needed to go through its past to get to the new album. And now that the Mael brothers have completed the process they have turned their history into a *now* and have no reason to do it again.

THE SECOND SET OF the night was nothing but rare cuts from their catalog. Supposedly chosen by the fans who entered their request on the Sparks website—it was an interesting collection of songs. It also ended the night with a sense of enjoyment and pleasure. The *Exotic Creatures* set, if it had ended the program, would have been a sad affair. Especially with Ron burning up the past Sparks' albums on the screen. The second set was basically a gift to the audience for sticking around for such a long time—both for the shows and the last forty-something years.

I SAW THE PRETTY bleach blonde girl who was at all the other shows alone. She was there with friends this time. The personality I had ascribed to her changed when I saw her with her pals. I had a whole imaginative life of this girl as a solitude figure, but no, she has friends. I guess what I saw in her was my loneliness. She wasn't lonely at all—she was having a blast. But me, I had to project my feelings on a perfect stranger. My reality has no bearing with anything out there. I thought of others in the audience, like the man who always read while waiting for Sparks to go onstage. He was there as well, but without a book. He looked like a different person from the other shows. He was alone, and now I think he probably works and always comes after his work, but who knows? I'm realizing that I've made up the lives of all these people; each is a figment of my imagination.

I gave up my life to come here, or rather put a hold on it. And now that my mission is over, I am feeling kind of lost. I spent over a month in London (and Paris) and I realized that I didn't go out to see people, except for those who I lived with—and that one time visiting the art curator. On an objective level, that solitude can be sad, but I love to be isolated while I'm watching

Sparks. At times I wanted to share my experience with Lun*na, but alas, my time was spent at the shows and in front of my computer laptop, writing my thoughts and feelings.

EARLIER, I WALKED AROUND Waterloo Bridge and went to check out the National Film Theatre. They totally revamped the whole building since I was there two years ago. They were playing Jean Renoir's last film *Le Petite Théâtre de Jean Renoir*, which by any means is not his best work, yet I was drawn to the first segment of the film called "Le dernier réveillon" about a tramp interacting with wealthy patrons at a restaurant. It starts off one way and then takes a left turn somewhere else.

The Tramp gets food (including champagne) from a very expensive restaurant and takes it back to his girlfriend. They eat and sort of imagine that they had a wealthy past, but the truth is that they have always been dirt poor and lived like tramps. They die in the snow without even eating their dinner. A flood of tears came out of my eyes in the darkened theater. I thought of Lun*na being so far away from me, I felt at that moment like a piece of trash floating in the ocean—going nowhere and just letting the currents take me to whatever is ahead. It struck me that I kept my emotions in place while on this trip. And Renoir's film just opened up something in me that I've been avoiding—missing my wife. I have basically been keeping myself busy on this trip to Europe. But for one moment, I allowed my mind to freely wander, and there we are, on the screen—frozen to death, yet happy.

This feeling came back to me several times while watching Sparks onstage. Sparks' songs elicited tears from me that I didn't know were waiting to be released. I don't think this is a normal reaction to the music by fans but my life is so intertwined with it. In a sense, I have known Sparks for thirty-four years, my entire adult life.

AFTERWORD: LOS ANGELES

have been back here in Los Angeles for almost two weeks, and my experiences in London seem like a dream where Peter Pan or Sparks picked me up from sleep and took me to Neverland. And then delivered me back to my bed before dawn.

Life seems boring now; my life seems divided into two periods, before twenty-one nights and after twenty-one nights. Angel, Islington, Upper Street, Holloway Road are the locations that I dream about at night.

RON AND RUSSELL HAVE lasted for twenty-one albums, and have been on almost every major label in the world—and yet, they've never had worldwide success. Most would have given up, but they are hungry for the thrill of making music, the success does not drive them.

London has always been the spiritual home to Sparks and its music. The Mael brothers have disappeared into the U.K. scene a few times, but they are always welcomed back with open arms. The American citizen usually complains about their fate as being unfair, seeing it as a right or wrong. The British perceive their fate as something truthful and right, so it would be wrong to think that they themselves can change their social or cultural identity. Sparks is similar to the British; they are destined to do what they have to do, and there is no question whether or not they can change their lives to something more comfortable or different. Sparks is a way of life.

THE TWENTY-ONE NIGHTS CARRY with them a sense of privacy that is almost church-like. Not in a worshiping sense, more in its solemnity. I never wanted to talk to the other fans in the audience, even those I saw on a daily basis. The guys who came from Germany, the French couple, Minnie Mouse, the yanks as well. All of us were part of an event, not a family.

BUT NOW THE SHOWS are over and I am back in my cave here in Los Angeles with my wife, my family. And in this moment, there is no place I'd rather be.

Tosh Berman
2008 -2012, Los Angeles, London,
Paris, Bushwick, and Tokyo

LIVE! 21 ALBUMS IN 21 NIGHT

SPAR

DOORS OPEN AT 19:00   www.allsparks.com

SPECTACULAR

AT CARLING ACADEMY ISLINGTON N1 CENTRE ISLINGTON LONDON N1 0PS

MAY

16 Halfnelson/Sparks (1971/2)
17 A Woofer In Tweeter's Clothing (1972)
SOLD OUT Kimono My House (1974)
SOLD OUT Propaganda (1974)
21 Indiscreet (1975)
23 Big Beat (1976)
24 Introducing Sparks (1977)
25 No. 1 In Heaven (1979)
27 Terminal Jive (1980)
28 Whomp That Sucker (1981)
30 Angst In My Pants (1982)
31 In Outer Space (1983)

JUNE

01 Pulling Rabbits Out Of A Hat (1984)
03 Music That You Can Dance To (1986)
04 Interior Design (1988)
06 Gratuitous Sax & Senseless Violins (1994)
07 Plagiarism (1997)
08 Balls (2000)
10 Lil' Beethoven (2002)
11 Hello Young Lovers (2006)

JUNE 13TH
WORLD PREMIERE OF SPARKS' 21ST ALBUM
'EXOTIC CREATURES OF THE DEEP'
LONDON SHEPHERDS BUSH EMPIRE
WWW.SHEPHERDS-BUSH-EMPIRE.CO.UK

TICKETS: 0844 477 2000 or Online @ www.ticketweb.co.uk www.academy-events.co.uk
Individual ticket price £20. show 3 nights or more £18 show. Golden ticket - all 21 shows £250 enticate PE